THE
S·C·E·N·T·E·D
HOUSE

Creating beautiful and naturally fragrant accessories
for every room in the house

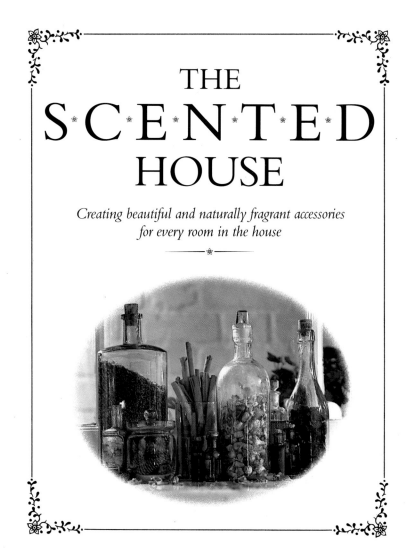

THE
S·C·E·N·T·E·D
HOUSE

PENNY BLACK

*Creating beautiful and naturally fragrant accessories
for every room in the house*

Photography by Geoff Dann

SIMON AND SCHUSTER
New York • London • Toronto • Sydney • Tokyo • Singapore

In memory of my darling mother, whose passion for cottages and gardens has become my own.

Important Notice

The recipes in this book are perfectly safe when properly mixed.
However, some of the ingredients may cause allergic reactions in some
individuals so reasonable care in the preparations is advised.

A DORLING KINDERSLEY BOOK

SIMON AND SCHUSTER
Simon & Schuster Building
Rockefeller Center
1230 Avenue of the Americas
New York, New York 10020

Copyright © 1990 by Dorling Kindersley
Limited, London
Text Copyright © 1990 by Penny Black

All rights reserved
including the right of reproduction
in whole or in part in any form.

SIMON AND SCHUSTER and colophon are
registered trademarks
of Simon & Schuster Inc.

First published in Great Britain in 1990 by
Dorling Kindersley Limited
9 Henrietta Street, London WC2E 8PS

ART EDITOR CAROLINE MULVIN
PROJECT EDITOR JO WEEKS
MANAGING ART EDITOR ALEX ARTHUR
MANAGING EDITOR JANE LAING
CONSULTING EDITOR MARTINA D'ALTON

Color reproduction by Colourscan, Singapore
Printed in Italy by A. Mondadori Editore, Verona
1 3 5 7 9 10 8 6 4 2

Library of Congress Cataloging in Publication Data
Black, Penny.
    The Scented House : creating beautiful and naturally fragrant
accessories for every room in the house / Penny Black ; photography
by Geoff Dann.
        p.   cm.
    "A Dorling Kindersley book"--T.p. verso.
    ISBN 0–671–70522–9
    1. Potpourris (Scented floral mixtures) 2. Handicraft.
I. Title.
TT899.4.B58 1991
745.92--dc20

90-34932
CIP

Contents

INTRODUCTION

❀

Of all the five senses there is none that stimulates the imagination more than that of smell. The subconscious memory is steeped in perfume and the merest drift of scent can evoke vivid recollections of sensations long since forgotten. More than all others it is the familiar scents of childhood that capture our imagination and transport us back to those early years. Who can smell a garden after summer rain without basking in its comforting sweetness? And who cannot find solace in the scented flowers of dusk and night?

❀ FLOWER ARRANGEMENTS *Dried flower arrangements can be large and flamboyant (right) or small and subtle (above). They are always an attractive decoration for the home.*

My own childhood memories are infused with the rich smells of the country and through them I am taken back to Dorsetshire fields, woods and hedgerows, to our garden and the humble little thatched cottage where I lived. In the woods nearby lingered the seductive Eastern perfume of honeysuckle, whose pale, nectared flowers so beguilingly projected their fragrance at the close of the day.

❧ BLUEBELLS & PRIMROSES ❧

There were juicy-stemmed bluebells, whose evocative sweet perfume is reminiscent of blue skies and warm summer sun, and delicate pallid primroses, whose mossy scent is the language of childhood. On dry banks grew aromatic cushions of thyme and in the wetland watermint guarded her secret fragrance until her downy leaves were trampled upon. In the garden grew heady lilac, clove-scented rambler roses and aromatic lad's love. Lily-of-the-valley filled shady corners and provided sweet white bells to perfume nosegays and buttonholes. Inside the cottage scented smoke from

burning apple logs, oil lamps and beeswax candles hung in the air, the tangy aroma of boiling marmalade and fresh mint sauce often filled the kitchen and from the medicine chest came the vaporous smell of friar's balsam and camphorated oil. On warm summer nights the exquisite perfume of jasmine drifted gently through my bedroom window.

For thousands of years fragrant flowers, leaves, roots, seeds, woods and resins have been used to scent our homes, food, clothes as well as ourselves. As we gradually became aware of the soothing and sybaritic properties of perfume, more sophisticated means were found to capture the many aromas of the natural world.

❧ THE ORIGINS OF PERFUME ❧

It was probably the scented smoke of burning wood that first alerted our senses to the pleasure of perfume for the word "perfume" is derived from *per fumin,* meaning "by means of smoke."

The Egyptians were the first to record the art of perfumery and it became an integral part of their everyday life. The perfumed resins of frankincense and myrrh were burned as fragrant offerings to the gods and the temples were heavy with their sweetness. With the discovery that many aromatics possess both germicidal and preservative properties, embalming, or mummification, became part of the Egyptian burial ritual. Scented cedar wood was used in the making of coffins, and the dead were buried with a fascinating array of fragrant unguents and oils. Elaborately perfumed preparations were massaged into the body and scented cosmetics

were used to rejuvenate and enhance facial beauty; there were even recipes for primitive deodorants. Bowls of scented botanicals perfumed rooms, as did burning incense. Frankincense, myrrh, sandalwood, calamus, cassia, cinnamon, peppermint, juniper, henna, orris and sweet herbs are just a few of the aromatics that were used. All of them are familiar and found in many of the recipes in this book. Many of them were carried to Egypt by Ishmaelite traders who ran the gauntlet of the ancient caravan routes to trade their spices and resins in the Land of the Pharoahs.

✧ PERFUME IN EUROPE ✧

The civilizations of the ancient Western world gained their knowledge of perfumery through the Egyptians. The Greeks often referred to perfume in their writings on mythology and all of their religious ceremonies involved the burning of incense and herbs. Highly fragrant cosmetics were used and herbal medicine was practiced.

The Romans learnt the aesthetic appreciation of scent and the art of perfumery from the Greek colonists of southern Italy. Following the fall of the Roman Empire European interest in perfumery declined and only the Christian church preserved the ancient rituals of incense burning and those that involved the use of fragrant oils. During the Dark Ages it was  the monasteries that cultivated aromatic flowers and herbs, but not for the use of making perfumes, rather for preparing herbal remedies and medicines.

✧ THE PERFECTION OF DISTILLATION ✧

However, during this period, the Arabs continued their research into the properties of fragrant plant materials and in the eleventh century the Arabian doctor Avicenna perfected the science of distillation.

Avicenna distilled the "attar", or essential oil, from the rose. This oil remains the most historic and important essential oil and is known as the "attar of roses."

✧ THE CRUSADERS & PERFUMERY ✧

The Crusaders revived the lost art of perfumery in Europe when they returned from the eastern Mediterranean, bringing with them many exquisitely perfumed toiletries and exciting new aromatics.

By the sixteenth century most large houses grew herbs and scented flowers – particularly roses – in their gardens. They were gathered by the mistress of the house and taken to her "still-room" – a room apart from the kitchen where a stove kept the atmosphere warm and dry. They were dried and stored there together with the many imported herbs and spices that were available. Oils, fats and lards, lanolin, beeswax and precious animal fixatives added to the fascinating contents of the room. One can imagine the delectable and curious scents that filled the air. Here the housewife dispensed all the cosmetics, cleaners and medicines that were essential to the well-being of her family and the sweetness of her home.

❈ SCENTED DECORATION *The fragrant winter-leaf potpourri in the patchwork cushion (above) will fill the living room with an intriguing perfume. The lovely bedroom garland (left), hung over a bed-post, will imbue the room with a delicate scent.*

✧ ROOM SWEETENERS ✧

Large bundles of herbs were prepared for strewing on the floors and fumigating the rooms. Scented pastilles and incense cones were made to sweeten the air, as were rich moist potpourris. Fragrant and moth-repellent fillings were made for sachets, which were then used to perfume and protect clothes and linen. Aromatic pomanders and spikenard, rosemary and lavender beads were fashioned from gums, resins, fixatives and essential oils; they perfumed the air and their germicidal properties helped to ward off infection. Delicately scented

washballs, soaps, colognes, floral waters, oils and other preparations were made for cosmetic use.

⚜ EXOTIC AROMATICS ⚜

With the advancement of scientific research many changes took place in the world of perfumery between the seventeenth and twentieth centuries. The scents of the fragrant flowers, leaves, woods and spices of the New World became more readily available: rhodium, cascarilla, sassafras, allspice, balsam of Peru, tonka and vanilla are a few of the poetically named aromatics from the Americas and West Indies. French and British perfumers of the nineteenth century sold an incredible assortment of fragrant colognes, soaps, pomades and oils, hair dyes and depilatories.

The twentieth century brought many changes, including the introduction of chemical fragrances, and gradually the diversity of the perfumer's preparations diminished. Potpourri, scented sachets and natural-beauty products temporarily fell out of fashion as we became reliant on artificially scented products. Today, however, we are once again eager to perfume our homes and ourselves with the lovely natural fragrances that captivated our ancestors.

⚜ THE ROSE ⚜

Look to the Rose that blows about us – "Lo,
Laughing," she says, "into the World I blow:
At once the silken tassel of my Purse
Tear, and its Treasure on the Garden throw"
From the Rubaiyat of Omar Khayyám

The unique role of the rose in perfumery has been, and remains of immense importance. The Egyptians adored it and it was sacred to their Goddess Isis. The fragrance of the rose contributed to their religious and domestic perfumery and was so much in demand that they exported roses made from fragments of wood, paper and cloth, after scenting them with rose oil. The Greeks and the Romans used the perfume of the rose in

❀ CHAIR CUSHION *In the filling of this lovely cushion (above), spicy, woody and floral scents are blended to produce a wonderful perfume.*

oils, unguents and essences and its petals were strewn on floors, used to fill mattresses and pillows and scattered on the living and over the tombs of the dead. Rose water even played in their fountains! In this book roses or rose oil are used in most recipes. The "rose leaves" referred to in many recipes in the old herbals are actually rose petals.

⚜ ESSENTIAL OILS ⚜

Essential oils are found in all aromatic plant materials: they give the flowers, leaves, seeds, roots, woods, resins and balsams their fragrance. Distillation is the most usual method of separating the oils from the plant materials. During this process the plant materials are saturated with steam from boiling water, making their fragrant oils evaporate. The resulting vapor mixes with the steam, and as the steam condenses the oil separates from it and floats on the surface. It can then be collected and bottled.

Another method of removing fragrant oils is extraction. This involves infusing the botanicals in either a fixed solvent of fat or oil, or a volatile solvent such as ether. Oils may also be obtained by expression, whereby pressure is applied to the leaves and flowers to squeeze out the oils.

The names of most essential oils are straightforward; here are some that are more misleading: *Neroli* – from the blossoms of the sweet orange, *Petitgrain* – from the twigs and leaves of the bitter orange tree, *Orange* – from the peel of the bitter orange, *Bergamot* – from the peel of the bergamot orange, *Bergamot mint* – from the leaves of the bergamot mint, *Monarda* – from the flowers and leaves of bergamot (*Monarda didyma*), *Ambrette* – from musk seeds.

⚜ FIXATIVES ⚜

Fixatives play an essential role in perfumery, for they fix or hold, the fragrance of the volatile essential-oils contained in the scented plant materials. Without fixatives perfume quickly loses its fragrance. Fixatives are often aromatic and their scent will add to the bouquet of a perfume.

Fixative properties are found in certain gums, resins, flowers, leaves, roots, seeds, spices, herbs and even lichens. In this book I have used orris root powder or finely ground gum benzoin because they are readily available. But you can use oakmoss, crumbled cinnamon sticks, sweet Cicely, angelica, coriander and cumin seeds, crushed tonka beans, chopped roots of sweet flag and elecampane, crumbled leaves of melilot or woodruff and finely ground resins of myrrh, galbanum and labdanum. If a dry fixative is not appropriate, oil of sandalwood, clove, cassia, cedarwood or patchouli may be used.

♪ A MEDLEY OF SCENTED DELIGHTS ♪

The Scented House is filled with both traditional and innovative ways of perfuming every room in the house. Some of the fragrant delights are steeped in antiquity, whilst others are my own ideas. Any natural, absorbent material can easily be impregnated with

❀ LAVENDER BASKET *(above) Decorations of pink and white flowers emphasize the beautiful simplicity of this display of mainly blues and grays.*

scent, giving immense scope to the field of creative perfumery. I use dried plant materials as an exciting medium with which to create intricate botanical embroideries and patchworks. The fragrance of a summer garden pervades the pressed- and dried-flower collages, while the aroma of herbs and the sweet fragrance of the rose lingers in the stationery. I love embroidery, fine sewing and old textiles and, when making scented pillows, cushions and sachets, I always consider both their fragrance and appearance. Even the bottles that contain my colognes, oils and sweet waters are decorated with sprigs of flowers and herbs. My home is a feast of visual pleasure and all the scented accessories in this book reflect my interest in the decorative arts as well as in perfumery.

The Hall & Stairs

THE HALL SETS THE SCENE for the entire home, and what could be more welcoming than a seductive fragrance. On entering the visitor immediately searches for the source of the perfume and derives much pleasure from the discovery of a basket or bowl brimming with potpourri, or an aromatic garland behind the door or looped over the newel post of the stairs. There are many garland bases available and when they are decorated with dried flowers, leaves, fruit, whole spices, mosses and lichen, their romantic charm always adds interest to any interior. Pretty old hats and bonnets, stuffed with sweet herbs and flowers, are a delightful decoration. One used to be able to obtain scented pictures from the East, with hollow frames which were filled with spicy aromatics. Although these are no longer available you can easily re-create them by rubbing wooden picture frames with the essential oil of cloves, cinnamon, nutmeg, sandalwood or cedarwood. Gentle, subtle perfumes are best for the hall and stairs as they will not spread to overwhelm the scents in other rooms. Colors should be warm and welcoming. The browns of woods and spices and the subdued pinks, mauves and blues of cottage garden flowers are ideal. Aromatic woods can often be collected on a woodland walk. Fir needles are easily discovered as are conifer foliage and fir cones, the refreshing scent of which can be strengthened by dropping a little pine oil into their centers. Sharpen woody scents with the intriguing perfume of bergamot orange. The shadowy fragrance of the rose is always welcome. Mix it with sweet herbs to produce a very lovely traditional fragrance.

❀ GARLANDS & COLLAGES *Unusual garlands (left) and delicately scented collages (above) are wonderful decorations for the hall and stairs.*

❧ FLORAL HOOPS ❧

CONSIDER CAREFULLY the colors and scents to use in your floral decorations for the hall, as they will be the first decorations a visitor to your house will encounter and they are therefore bound to make a significant impression. Shades of brown and green and woody or spicy scents are ideal as they empathize with the world outside, so close at hand. If you have also made potpourris for the hall, ensure that their scents and colors complement those of the garlands. In addition to the wall, you might also like to hang a garland on the newel at the end of the banisters or on the inner side of the front door. Enhance or refresh the scent of a garland by rubbing perfumed oil into the willow base or by periodically spraying the base or the flowers with perfume.

LILAC

POTENTILLA

✿ SEMI-BASKET *Flowers and other plant materials, scented with essential oils and glued to a cardboard backing, produce a fine display for this two-dimensional garland.*

EVERLASTING FLOWERS

ROSE

❀ MOSSY GARLAND
*Browns, creams, grays
and greens are used
to give this garland a
muted appearance. A
lovely scent is produced
by the sandalwood oil,
which has been dropped on
the oakmoss and the pine
cones, and the whole spices.*

FIR CONE

CINNAMON STICK

WHEAT EAR

NUTMEG

❀ DELICATE CIRCLET
*Rose oil and myrrh oil
have been dropped into
the center of each of
the roses to imbue this
dainty circlet with a
wonderful perfume
that is both ancient
and evocative.*

QUEEN-ANNE'S-
LACE

GLOBE AMARANTH

❀ SCENTED BASKET
This beautiful dried-flower display, arranged in an aromatic, vetiver basket has an unusual fragrance of orange and frankincense.

❀ SHOE CLEANING BOX
Painted matte-black and edged with gold leaf, this unusual container is filled with a rich and spicy Elizabethan potpourri of roses and herbs.

❀ INGREDIENTS
(LEFT): ANAPHALIS (DYED PINK), DOUBLE DAISY, GYPSOPHILA, LARKSPUR, POTENTILLA, ROSE, ROSE BUDS, ROSE PETALS AND VERBENA.

❧ POTPOURRIS ❧

Woody scents are particularly appropriate for the hall, making a gentle transition from the outside to the inside world. Old-fashioned domestic containers, such as tea caddies, cookie jars, sewing boxes, chocolate boxes, hat boxes and even shoe boxes, can be used for displaying potpourri, often with marvelous results. Use the hall table, the floor, the stairs, the wall or a coat hook to present your potpourri.

❀ INGREDIENTS (LEFT): ABUTILON, LAVENDER, LILAC, MALLOW, POTENTILLA, QUEEN-ANNE'S-LACE ROSE AND ROSE PETALS.

❀ WOODEN BOWL *The emphasis is on texture in this heady, woody potpourri. Potentillas and delphiniums add splashes of color.*

❀ INGREDIENTS (RIGHT): CINNAMON STICK, CLOVES, CORK SHAVINGS, DELPHINIUM, FIR CONE, NUTMEG, POTENTILLA, SENNA PODS, STAR ANISE, STAR TILIA AND WOOD SHAVING.

❧ FLORAL WALL HANGINGS ❧

THE LARGE AREA OF WALL SPACE in the hall and by the side of the stairs is ideal for displaying hanging scented decorations. Eye-catching arrangements for these positions can take almost any form you like. Try decorating objects that are usually found in the hall, such as the coat rack or an umbrella stand, or make just one bold design that will act as a focal point. As the hall and stairs are generally quite airy, make the scent fairly strong but not so powerful that it spreads throughout the rest of the house and overwhelms the perfumes in other rooms. Woody scents are very effective in the hall or, for a more refreshing fragrance, try mixing citrus peel with herbs.

✽ HEART OF HOPS
& HEATHER
Visually stunning, although simple in design, this rich purple and pale green heart is scented with a potpourri reviver.

❀ POSY OF
PRESSED
FLOWERS *This
tiny, pressed-
flower bouquet is
bordered with a
gilt frame. The back
of the frame has been
rubbed with oil of
cloves, so that the
picture exudes a strong
but simple fragrance.*

❀ EDWARDIAN HAT *Decorated
with dried flowers and filled with
potpourri, this lovely hat
exudes the rich fragrance
of scented woods and
bergamot orange.*

❧ RECIPES ❧

POTPOURRIS FOR DISPLAY

SWEET MIX

2pt (1 liter) MIXED SCENTED FLOWERS
2oz (60g) ROSEMARY
1oz (30g) ORRIS ROOT POWDER
$^{1}/_{2}$ CHOPPED VANILLA POD
2 TONKA BEANS
2 TEASPOONS GRATED NUTMEG
2 DROPS CARNATION OIL
2 DROPS NEROLI OIL
2 DROPS ROSEMARY OIL

This sweet but subtle dry potpourri is lovely in the hall and stairs area.

WOODY MIX

1pt (500ml) MIXED SCENTED WOODS
1pt (500ml) MIXED OF ANY OF THE FOLLOWING — BERRIES, CORK SHAVINGS, FIR CONES, NUTMEGS, SENNA PODS & STAR TILIA
1oz (30g) ROSEMARY
1oz (30g) ORRIS ROOT POWDER
3 CINNAMON STICKS
3 STAR ANISE
4 TONKA BEANS
3 DROPS CEDARWOOD OIL
3 DROPS SANDALWOOD OIL
1 DROP FRANKINCENSE OIL
PINK POTENTILLA
& BLUE DELPHINIUM
FLOWERS TO DECORATE

*The **Wooden Bowl** (p.17) displays this woody-scented dry potpourri, which is ideal for the hall. It has a heady fragrance that is strong enough to perfume a large area but is not too pervasive.*

ELIZABETHAN MIX

2pt (1 liter) MIXED PINK & BLUE FLOWERS
2oz (60g) MIXED SWEET HERBS
1oz (30g) LAVENDER
1oz (30g) FINE-GROUND GUM BENZOIN
2 TEASPOONS CRUSHED ALLSPICE BERRIES
1 TEASPOON CLOVES
1 CRUMBLED CINNAMON STICK
4 DROPS ELIZABETHAN POTPOURRI OIL
2 DROPS CLOVE OIL
WOODRUSH FLOWERHEADS TO DECORATE

*The **Shoe Cleaning Box** (p.16) is filled with this old-fashioned dry potpourri. It is a lovely mix, ideal for filling the hall and stairs area with a gentle scent.*

❋ WOODY MIX *The most suitable potpourris for the hall and stairs are those that contain woody ingredients. This mix is perfect as it combines the lovely warm colors and textures of woody pine cones, nutmegs, star anise and star tilia with the brighter colors of potentilla and delphinium flowers.*

TANGY ROSE MIX

1pt (500ml) Mixed Whole Roses
& Rose Petals
1pt (500ml) Mixed Garden Flowers
1oz (30g) Lemon Verbena
1oz (30g) Lavender
1oz (30g) Orris Root Powder
2 Teaspoons Cinnamon Powder
1 Teaspoon Cloves
1 Teaspoon Coriander Seeds
4 Drops Orange Oil
2 Drops Frankincense Oil
Bunch of Lavender to Decorate

*The **Scented Basket** (pp.16-17) displays
this dry potpourri. The orange and
frankincense oils lend it a deep, tangy
fragrance that is sweetened and
softened by the roses.*

FIR CONE MIX

2pt (1 liter) Mixed Fir Cones
2 or 3 Small Citrus Pomanders
(optional)
1oz (30g) Lavender
1oz (30g) Fine-ground Gum Benzoin
1 Chopped Vanilla Pod
2 Teaspoons Allspice Berries
4 Drops Juniper Oil
2 Drops Lemon Oil
2 Drops Orange Oil

*This is a lovely highly textured
dry potpourri, ideal for displaying
in the hall and
stairs area.*

AUTUMN BERRY
& LEAF MIX

1pt (500ml) Brightly Colored
Autumn Leaves (gathered
before they fall & very
lightly pressed for
2 or 3 days)
1pt (500ml) Mixed Hips,
Haws & Berries
1oz (30g) Lavender
1oz (30g) Fine-ground
Gum Benzoin
4 Tonka Beans
2 Broken Cinnamon Sticks
1 Teaspoon Cloves
4 Drops Rhodium Oil
2 Drops Myrrh Oil
2 Drops Rose Oil

*The lovely bright colors of
autumn are captured in this
dry potpourri.*

POTPOURRIS FOR
CONTAINERS

BERGAMOT ORANGE &
SANDALWOOD MIX

1pt (500ml) Sandalwood Shavings
1pt (500ml) Bergamot Leaves
2oz (60g) Lavender
1oz (30g) Orris Root Powder
Grated Rind
of an Orange
2 Teaspoons Crushed
Allspice Berries
1 Teaspoon
Cinnamon Powder
4 Drops Sandalwood Oil
2 Drops Bergamot Oil

*The **Edwardian Hat** (p.19) is
stuffed with this dry potpourri.
Bergamot orange and sandalwood
combine to produce a delicious
fragrance. Fill the crown of the
hat with the potpourri. Keep it
in place with a circle of net,
slightly larger that the base
of the crown, loosely
tacked in place.*

The Living Room

Of all the rooms in the house, the living room is the best place to display your most lavish perfumed achievements. Pressed-flower pictures, using the scented flowers of a summer garden or an array of old roses, surrounded by a mixed border of flowers, are lovely. Use scented paper as a base or perfume the flowers so that the air around the collage is infused with fragrance. If you have the space, a large basket filled with fascinating aromatics might make the most intriguing feature in the room. Be imaginative when displaying potpourri. Bowls, jars, dishes and baskets of fragrant mixes can be placed almost anywhere. Create immense impact by filling an old wooden rocking cradle, a chest or a dough bin with a magnificent display of dried roses, peonies, tulips and any other rich and flamboyant flowers. Make appliqué and

✿ MIXED FRAGRANCES *A large dried-flower bouquet (left) or a diffuser full of moist potpourri (above) will fill the room with a lovely blend of scents.*

patchwork cushions and sachets from scraps of fabric and lace, or create frilled and piped cushions from a fabric that matches or coordinates with the other soft furnishings in the room. If the fragrant delights are to be displayed over a large area, scent them with different mixes, although be careful not to make them too overpowering. Just a little myrrh frankincense or patchouli will add a rich and soothing touch to the lighter fragrances of lavender, geranium, rose and tangy orange. The perfumes of fragrant woods and seeds have a unique softness that blends well with almost all other scents. Of course, you may well prefer to use quite different perfumes in your living room than those suggested. It is all a matter of personal choice, and you can have great fun experimenting to discover what appeals most.

CUSHIONS

SWEETLY PERFUMED cushions are a delightful way to scent the living room. Use pretty scraps of linen, lace and fabric to make opulent appliqué cushions or more humble patchwork ones – whichever suits the room. Fabrics that coordinate with other soft furnishings are also appropriate. Choice of scent is highly personal and can vary from light perfumes to luxuriant aromas.

PATCHWORK & APPLIQUE
These lightly scented, hand-worked cushions are ideal for informal rooms.

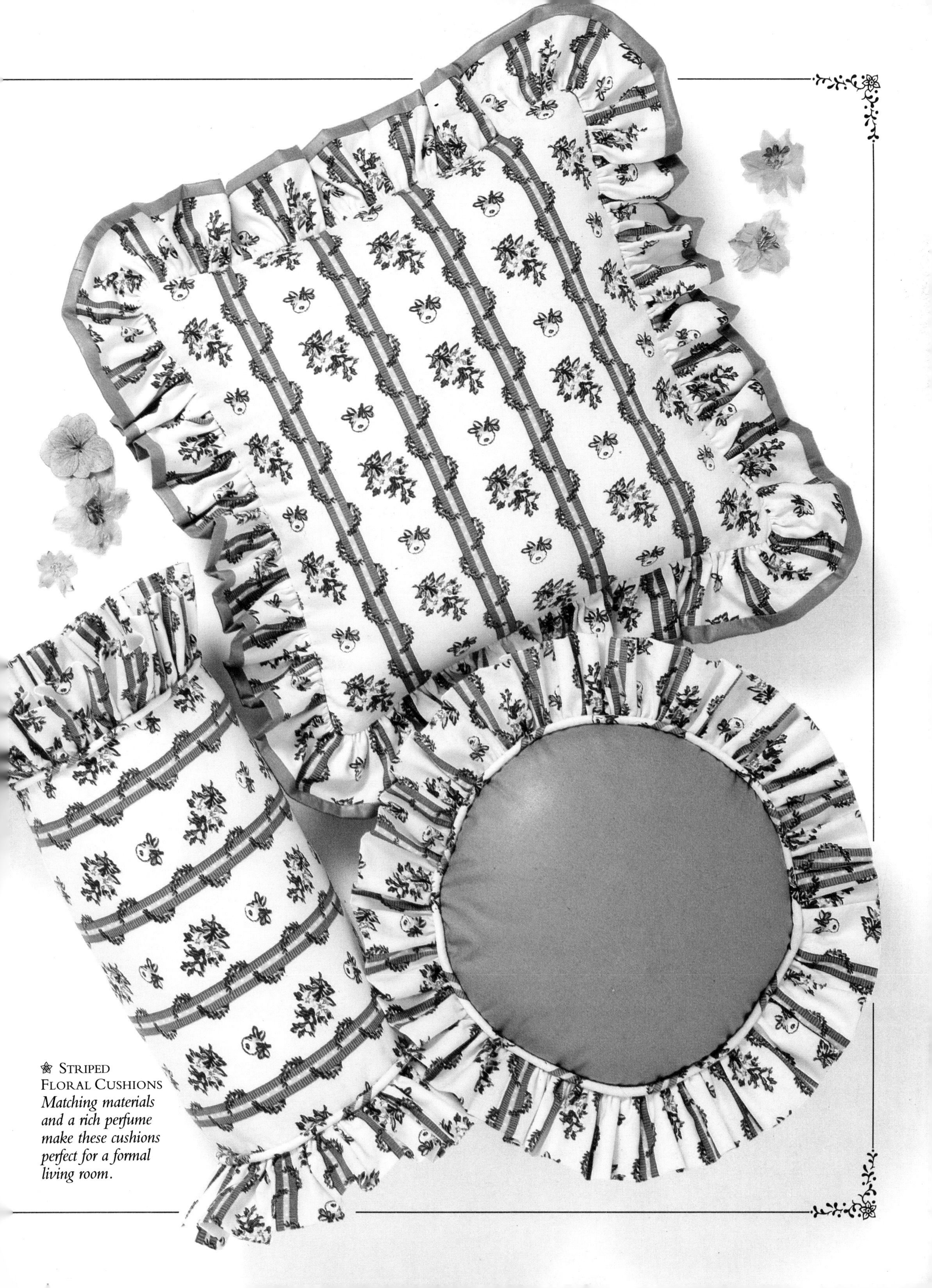

❀ STRIPED
FLORAL CUSHIONS
*Matching materials
and a rich perfume
make these cushions
perfect for a formal
living room.*

✤ PATCHWORK SQUARES
*These square sachets,
carefully trimmed with
lace and ribbon, and
filled with a sweet wood
potpourri, should be
displayed in a
prominent position
where their intricate
designs can be seen
to advantage.*

✤ AROMATIC
HEART *Filled with
mixed aromatic seeds,
this rich red heart makes a
lovely, luxurious decoration.*

❧ PETITE SACHETS ❧

SMALL SACHETS, filled with herbs and scented mixes, will fill the living room with a subtle fragrance. Suspend them from small hooks on the bookcase, doorknobs, radiators, curtain rails and curtain rods; tuck them into the sides of chairs and sofas; or lay them on a flat surface, such as a coffee table. Wherever you place them, they are bound to be appreciated for their delicate appearance and their subtle fragrance. Make individual sachets using small scraps of material remaining from other projects, or use the same material as seat cushions to make an attractive set of color-coordinated soft furnishings. Even fragile laces and silks can be used if backed with iron-on interfacing. The shape you choose to make your sachets is a matter of individual preference. Size is also dependent on taste but be sure that they are small enough to be dainty and elegant. Try making several tiny sachets and link them together on a wooden ring, or make a larger sachet and decorate it with embroidery or lace.

❀ TUBULAR POUCHES
A pair of slim sachets, exuding a woody rose scent are perfect for placing in drawers.

❀ SPHERICAL SACHETS *These little bags hang together on a fine wooden ring to make an unusual decoration, suitable for tying to the end of a curtain rod.*

❀ APPLIQUE LACE BAG
Trimmed with delicate, cream lace, this little bag exudes a fragrance of orange and patchouli.

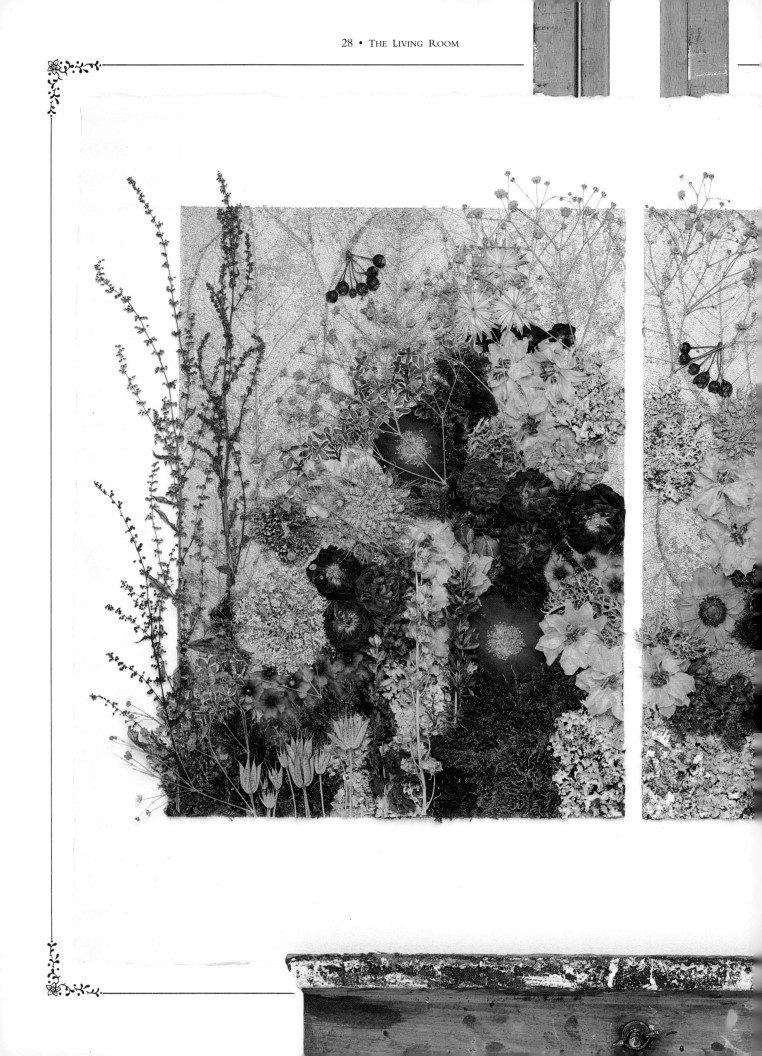

Denny Black Apr. '97

❧ GARDEN COLLAGE ❧

Elegant, scented, pressed-flower collages provide a delightful way to perfume a room gently as their shadowy fragrance is distinct only when you pass close by. To make the most impact, large collages must have plenty of wall space; smaller ones are less dominant and look delightful displayed with other pictures. You can make these pictures almost exclusively from aromatic botanicals, although it is sometimes preferable to scent the paper before starting on the design. Alternatively, if you are using a wooden frame, you might like to rub an essential oil into the back.

— CREATING A COLLAGE —

Creating a collage presents endless possibilities. Almost any pressed plant material can be used: mosses, lichens and fungi, weeds, herbs, spices, fruits, berries and seedheads, all garden flowers and even some seaweeds. Aromatic, whole spices, such as cloves, produce lovely, textural contrasts and add to the bouquet of the picture. Dried botanicals are subtly colored, so it is possible to mix many different hues without the risk of their clashing.

— FINDING INSPIRATION —

Inspiration can come from your own garden, or from anything that is ornamented: china, embroidery and textiles, paintings and illustrations, jewelry and even a sheet of gift wrapping paper. Re-create a summer flower border using elements in the way that they appear naturally, or try making your own abstract and geometric designs.

❀ SUMMER BORDER
Skeletonized leaves, sprayed silver-blue are the perfect backdrop for this lovely design. A drop of rose geranium oil, then a drop of clary sage oil is put in the center of each rose and the lichen is scented with 3 drops of frankincense oil. The resulting fragrance is very nostalgic.

❧ SINGLE ARRANGEMENTS ❧

I N THE LIVING ROOM, large and solitary aromatic arrangements are very effective, especially when displayed in a prominent position. If your living room is spacious and sparsely furnished, a large display will accentuate its elegance and grandeur, while a single, eye-catching but small-scale decoration can provide a small room, which may have a tendency to feel overcrowded, with the illusion of space. In large rooms, where space is not a problem, display your creation on the floor or on a side table, or make it the center of a larger display, surrounding it with smaller, complementary decorations. If you decide to create a large arrangement for a small living room, ensure that there is enough space to set it off and make it a focal point. A basket arrangement looks superb placed on the floor by the fireplace or on a windowsill.

– COLORS –

It is not essential to choose strong, sharp colors when creating large arrangements for the living room as their size alone will ensure that they are eye-catching. A very striking idea is to use mainly subtle or muted colors but also to include one or two brighter colors in order to lift the display.

– SCENTS –

Depending on taste, scent can range from the simple to the sophisticated. Often large decorations are most effective if the fragrance is fairly light but comprises a mixture of perfumes.

✿ BASKET OF
FRAGRANCE *This
basket is filled with a
delectable assortment of
plant materials, including
bundles of cinnamon sticks,
lavender twigs, orris root,
driftwood scented with essential
oil, and several types of fir cone.
The various elements are arranged in
informal groups, thus emphasizing the
contrasts of color, texture and shape. The
whole basket exudes a bouquet of subtle perfumes.*

❧ POTPOURRIS ❧

IN THE LIVING ROOM, many surfaces can be used for displaying bowls of potpourri, including coffee tables, bookshelves, floors and windowsills. The range of scents is also wide. Decide what sort of atmosphere you wish to produce and then give your creativity a free rein. Try unusual color combinations like sea-green and slate-blue, and experiment with different textures, such as papery, satin-smooth roses combined with rough fronds of lichen.

❋ INGREDIENTS: ANAPHALIS, HYDRANGEA, LARKSPUR, OAKMOSS AND WATER FORGET-ME-NOT.

❋ LITTLE BLUE VASE *The strong perfume of rose and frankincense permeates through the decorative top layer of this moist potpourri.*

❋ INGREDIENTS: ANAPHALIS (DYED PINK AND JADE), GYPSOPHILA, LAVENDER, DAMASK ROSE AND PEACH ROSE.

❊ ALMOND-GREEN BOWL
In this potpourri (left) the brown
of the cinnamon blends with the
pink of the roses, and the gray-
green of the oakmoss matches
the bowl. The scent is a
light fragrance of mint
and rose.

❊ DECORATIVE ISLAMIC BOWL
An Eastern influence is clear in the
color scheme of this mix, from the
Damask rose in the center to the dyed
jade anaphalis around the edge. The
scent is suitably oriental, combining
tea tree oil with piquant
geranium oil.

❊ INGREDIENTS:
CINNAMON STICKS,
OAKMOSS, *ROSA MUNDI*,
ROSA 'FELICITE
PERPETUE', ROSE BUDS
AND RUGOSA ROSES.

❧ SCENTED STATIONERY ❧

PRESSED FLOWERS, glue and good-quality art paper are all that you require to make your own unique and charming cards, note paper, envelopes, bookmarks and gift tags. Perfume your stationery by storing it in a small box or a drawer along with a sachet of potpourri. Choose one of your favorite scents to perfume the paper and alter it whenever the mood takes you. Bookmarks can be scented with woodruff, which repels insects and is a time-honored protector of paper. Perfume your inks with a fragrant infusion – the traditional scent is patchouli – for a personal touch to your letters.

❀ PEN & INK *Scent your ink with heady patchouli.*

❀ CARDS & NOTE PAPER *These beautiful cards are imbued with the scent of lavender and decorated with pressed flowers.*

❀ WAXED CARDS *Rose-scented wax scents and protects the pressed flowers on these cards.*

❀ BOOKMARKS *Woodruff decorates and scents the bookmark on the right, that on the left is perfumed with a spicy clove mix.*

❀ GIFT TAGS *These tags are perfect for a special gift.*

❀ NOTE PAPER & ENVELOPES *Make matching writing paper, using one or two pressed flowers. Sandalwood perfumes this paper.*

❧ RECIPES ❧

POTPOURRIS FOR CUSHIONS

FRAGRANT WINTER LEAF MIX

2pt (1 liter) Mixed Scented Leaves
from the Winter Garden such as
Bog Myrtle, Box, Conifer Tips,
Eucalyptus, Hypericum, Jerusalem
Sage, Myrtle & Pine Needles
2oz (60g) Rosemary
1oz (30g) Orris Root Powder
2 Teaspoons Cloves
2 Broken Cinnamon Sticks
6 Drops Myrtle or Pine Oil
2 Drops Rosemary Oil

*The **Patchwork & Appliqué Cushions**
(p.24) are filled with this light, fresh
dry potpourri, which is ideal
for filling cushions.*

SPRING NOSEGAY MIX

2pt (1 liter) Mixed Scented
Spring Flowers such as
Hyacinths, Jonquils,
Lilies-of-the-Valley & Violets
2oz (60g) Lavender
1oz (30g) Orris Root Powder
2 Teaspoons Crushed Mace
Peel of $\frac{1}{2}$ an Orange
Peel of $\frac{1}{2}$ a Lemon
2 Drops Jonquil Oil
2 Drops Lavender or Violet Oil
2 Drops Lily-of-the-Valley Oil

*The **Striped Floral Cushions**
(p.25) are stuffed with this rich
dry potpourri that will fill the living
room with the scent of spring.*

❀ Applique Lace Bag
*This attractive appliqué lace
bag exudes the heady
fragrance of the
Patchouli, Jasmine
& Orange Mix.*

POTPOURRIS FOR SACHETS

WOODSY ROSE MIX

1pt (500ml) Rose Petals
1pt (500ml) Mixed Scented Woods
1oz (30g) Lavender
1oz (30g) Musk Seeds or
Chopped Eryngium Roots
2 Teaspoons Crushed
Coriander Seeds
2 Tonka Beans
4 Drops Rose Oil
2 Drops Cedarwood Oil

*The **Tubular Pouches** (p.27) are
filled with this dry potpourri. The
delicious musky fragrance of this mix
is lovely in the living room.*

SWEET WOOD MIX

2pt (1 liter) Mixed Scented Woods
such as Barberry Bark,
Cedarwood, Cinnamon Bark,
Cypress Wood, Logwood Chips,
Quassia Chips, Santal Wood,
Sandalwood, Sassafras
& Fragrant Sawdust
2oz (60g) Lavender
1oz (30g) Fine-ground
Gum Benzoin
2 Teaspoons Crushed
Allspice Berries
4 Star Anise
4 Drops Bois de Rose Oil
4 Drops Cypress Oil

*The **Log Cabin Squares** (p.26)
are filled with this pervading
woody-scented dry potpourri,
which is ideal for sachets.*

AROMATIC SEED MIX

2pt (1 liter) MIXED AROMATIC
SEEDS SUCH AS ALLSPICE,
ANGELICA, CARAWAY,
CARDAMOM, CORIANDER,
CUMIN, NUTMEG, STAR ANISE,
SWEET CECILY & TONKA BEANS
2oz (60g) ROSEMARY
1oz (30g) ORRIS ROOT POWDER
1oz (30g) CINNAMON POWDER
6 DROPS ANGELICA, CLARY SAGE OR MUSK
OIL
2 DROPS COSTUS
OR VIOLET OIL

*The **Aromatic Heart** (p.26) and
the **Spherical Sachets** (p.27) are
filled with this dry potpourri, which
has a spiced musky fragrance
strengthened by sweet violet oil.*

PATCHOULI, JASMINE & ORANGE MIX

1³/₄pt (875ml) JASMINE FLOWERS
¹/₄pt (125ml) ORANGE PEEL
2oz (60g) LAVENDER
1oz (30g) ORRIS ROOT POWDER
1 CHOPPED VANILLA POD
1 TEASPOON GRATED NUTMEG
4 DROPS JASMINE OIL
2 DROPS PATCHOULI OIL

*The **Appliqué Lace Bag** (p.27)
contains this dry potpourri. The
jasmine and patchouli in this luxuriant
mix produce a heady scent that is
sharpened by the tangy orange peel.*

✿ PATCHWORK
SQUARE *Filled
with Sweet Wood
Mix, this sachet is
perfect for displaying
in the living room.*

POTPOURRIS FOR DISPLAY

ELEGANT ROSE MIX

1pt (500ml) MIXED WHOLE ROSES
1pt (500ml) OAKMOSS
2oz (60g) DRIED MINT
1oz (30g) ORRIS ROOT POWDER
1 TEASPOON CRUSHED MACE
4 TONKA BEANS
4 BROKEN CINNAMON STICKS
RIND OF A LEMON
3 DROPS ROSE OIL
1 DROP LEMON OIL
1 DROP PEPPERMINT OIL

*The **Almond-green Bowl** (p.33)
displays this traditional dry potpourri.
Its scent is sweet but refreshing.*

ORIENTAL GERANIUM MIX

2pt (1 liter) MIXED SCENTED FLOWERS
2oz (60g) SCENTED GERANIUM
(PELARGONIUM) LEAVES
1oz (30g) FINE-GROUND GUM BENZOIN
2 TEASPOONS CINNAMON POWDER
¹/₂ GRATED NUTMEG
PEEL OF ¹/₂ AN ORANGE
PEEL OF ¹/₂ A LEMON
4 DROPS TEA TREE OIL
2 DROPS GERANIUM OIL
1 DROP PATCHOULI OIL
JADE- & PINK-DYED ANAPHALIS
& WHOLE ROSES TO DECORATE

*The **Islamic Bowl** (p.33) contains
this dry potpourri, which has an
intriguing oriental fragrance.*

HERBAL MIX

2pt (1 liter) STOCK-POT PETALS
2oz (60g) MIXED SWEET HERBS
1oz (30g) LEMON VERBENA
1oz (30g) OAKMOSS
1oz (30g) ORRIS ROOT POWDER
1 TEASPOON CINNAMON POWDER
1 TEASPOON CLOVES
1 TEASPOON GRATED LEMON RIND
4 DROPS GERANIUM OIL
2 DROPS FRANKINCENSE OIL
BLUE FLOWERS TO DECORATE

*The **Little Blue Vase** (p.32) contains
this rich and evocative moist potpourri.*

SCENTED INK

PATCHOULI INK

¹/₂pt (250ml) PATCHOULI LEAVES
³/₄pt (375ml) BOILING WATER

*Patchouli Ink (p.34). Place leaves
and water in a bowl. Leave for 2 hours
then strain into a pan. Boil until the
liquid is reduced by half. When cool,
add 1 teaspoon to 2fl oz (60ml) of ink.*

The Kitchen

Most kitchens enjoy a cornucopia of sweet-smelling ingredients. Cloves, cumin, allspice, coriander and many other spices are used extensively in today's cosmopolitan cuisine, as are many sweet herbs including marjoram thyme, sage and mint. Their delicious fragrance can also be used selectively in almost every potpourri, not to mention pomanders, collages and dried-flower displays. Try using more unusual aromatics, such as eucalyptus and myrtle leaves, lemon verbena, bergamot, feverfew, catmint and fluffy heads of Joe Pye weed, in kitchen potpourris, together with tangy citrus fruits. Shining brass and copper containers evoke the atmosphere of the kitchens of the past and look gorgeous crammed full of sweet-smelling, freshly picked herbs and perhaps some bunches of immature fruit.

✿ Fresh & Dried *Aromatic plants (left) and crushed spices (above) all add to the aromas of the kitchen.*

Alternatively, place an ample basket, laden with herbs and flowers in a warm, dry spot, where they will slowly desiccate. Add to the scents of the kitchen by hanging bunches of herbs to dry. Tansy, santolina, rosemary, thyme, southernwood and wormwood are especially useful as they also act as insect repellants. For the wall, make aromatic poster collages or a deep-framed picture, displaying an enticing array of flowers, herbs and spices, each element contained in its own compartment. Lastly, there are few things more pleasurable at the end of the day than the intimacy of a meal at the kitchen table under the soft, honeyed glow of fragrant candles. Ideal kitchen colors are verdant greens, bright yellows and oranges, red and the essential dash of blue.

❧ GATHERING FLOWERS & HERBS ❧

WHEN YOU HAVE SPENT TIME nurturing the herbs in your garden, it is infinitely satisfying to be able to collect some and bring them into the house so that you can continue to appreciate them when it is not possible to be outside. The best time to gather most herbs is in late summer when they are mature but have not yet begun to deteriorate. Evergreen herbs, such as rosemary and thyme, can be harvested at any time of the year, although it is best to allow new growth to harden before winter sets in. If you are picking the herbs for their leaves, it is best to do this in the morning immediately after the sun has evaporated the dew; gather the flowers at midday when they are fully opened.

— USING HERBS —

Arrange some fresh herbs in an attractive container to decorate the kitchen and to be within easy reach when they are needed for culinary purposes. Hang herbs that are not wanted for immediate use in bunches in a shady part of the room. Later they can be added to scented mixes or they can be crumbled and stored in jars for use in cooking in the winter.

❀ BUNCH FOR HANGING
*Two varieties of feverfew –
single- and semi-double-
flowering – together with
variegated mint make up
this simple herbal bouquet
secured with raffia. The
yellow centers of the
feverfew flowers are pretty
when dry. If the mint
is to be used in
cooking it should
be picked before
it flowers.*

❀ BASKET OF HERBS
*An English trug basket is
ideal for collecting flowers
and herbs. Its flat base allows
the plant material to lie together
loosely without being crushed, and
it is shallow, so the air can circulate
around the plants, keeping them
fresh until you are ready to remove
them. This attractive, rustic trug is
filled with eupatorium, bergamot,
marigolds, alchemilla, smallage,
sweet flag and artemisia.*

❧ FRESH HERB DISPLAYS ❧

SHINING BRASS AND COPPER KITCHEN CONTAINERS are perfect receptacles in which to arrange herbs. Here the interesting textures and lovely brilliant greens of the herbs contrast strongly with the smooth, metallic sheen of the kettle, jug and ship's water canister. A large number of these old-fashioned herbs, such as marjoram, smallage and fennel, are useful for flavoring food. Some have other household uses – soapwort is a washing agent and artemisia, when dried and crumbled, is a good moth repellant.

❀ SHIP'S WATER CANISTER
This unusual dispenser (right) is filled to overflowing with a wonderful assortment of plant material including astrantia, bistort, crab apples, double chamomile, euphorbia, fennel, feverfew, fleabane, Inula hookeri, I. magnifica, marjoram, meadowsweet, Polygonum campanulatum, St. Johnswort, smallage and variegated mint.

✿ COPPER JUG *Meadowsweet, fennel, soapwort, bergamot, smallage, astrantia, double chamomile, verbena, feverfew and* Inula hookeri *combine to create a striking arrangement in this bright copper jug (below left).*

✿ BRASS KETTLE *Containing stems of euphorbia, lemon balm, vervain, good King Henry, garden rue, lad's love, St. Johns wort, royal fern and purple sage, this brass kettle (below) is a charming vessel for such a display.*

❧ BOTANICAL POSTERS & SAMPLERS ❧

Intriguing and beautiful poster collages are easily made using the basic elements of perfumery. These basic elements include herbs, spices, gums, resins, seeds and barks, many of which are used in the kitchen, so it is the most appropriate room in which to display collages of this kind. Try producing a formal arrangement of herbs and spices, annotating the poster in the manner of an old botanical illustration. Another possibility is to take the delightful needlework samplers of the eighteenth and nineteenth centuries as your inspiration, and create a display of berries and lichen. subtle blend of pressed and scented flowers, herbs and whole spices, The fragrance produced by these posters is a the elements that have been used. If you wish to make the perfume more pronounced, scent the paper before you begin the design.

✿ TRADITIONAL DESIGNS
This herb poster (left) is annotated, giving it a traditional, botanical appearance. The lavish collage (right) is designed to be like a needlework sampler with plant materials replacing the embroidery stitches.

Hypericum Pulchrum   *Mentha Longifolia*

Borago officinalis   *Salvia officinalis*

Lavendula officinalis   *Myrrhis odorata*

Anthemis nobilis   *Polygonum distorta*

Foeniculum vulgare   *Myrtus communis*

Filipendula ulmaria   *Juniperus communis*

CINNAMON STICK

ORANGE PEEL

MINT

CONIFER

DOUBLE CHAMOMILE

MARJORAM

BORAGE

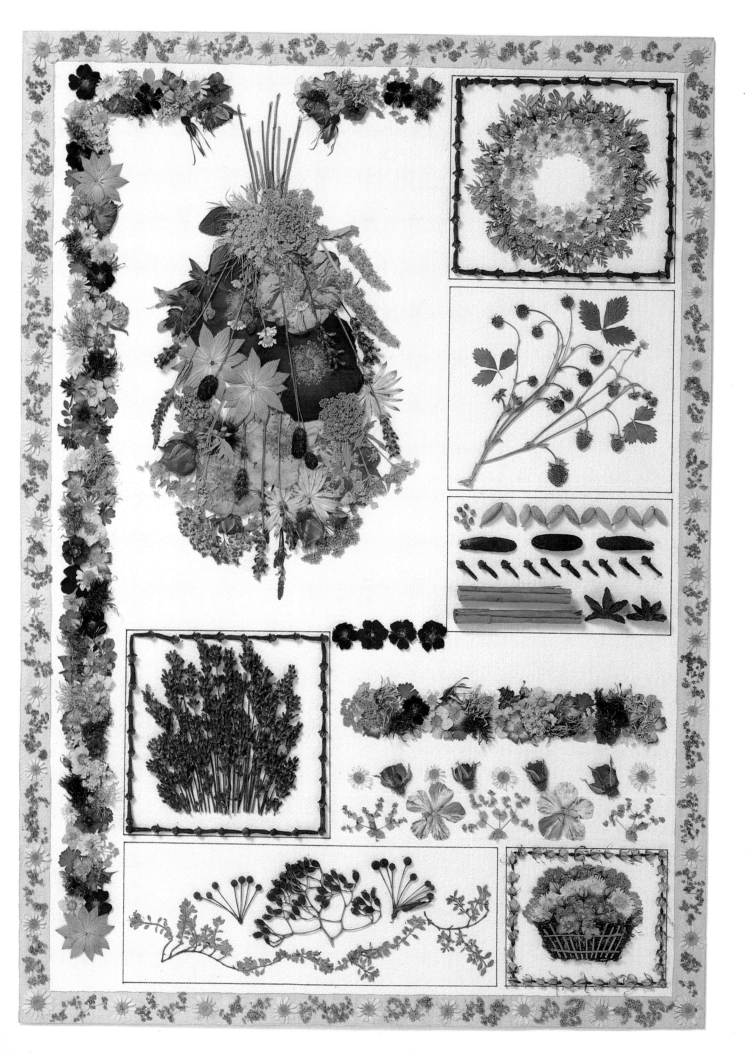

❧ BOLD DISPLAYS ❧

BOLD BUT SIMPLE SHAPES look stunning in the kitchen whether displayed singly or in groups, on the windowsill, the dresser or even the kitchen table. You can make a wonderful, self-contained decoration with just a few basic, kitchen-related elements. Alternatively, by using a wealth of plant material of many different hues, you can build up a tremendously exuberant and eye-catching display. Designs for the kitchen should always be bright and cheerful so the best colors to use are shades of orange, red, yellow and green. The most suitable scents for these displays are strong, but clean and crisp, and, once again, associated with the kitchen. Spicy or fruity fragrances, for example, will blend in with cooking smells and refresh the kitchen when preparations for the meal are complete.

❀ CITRUS POMANDERS
Oranges, lemons and grapefruit pierced with cloves exude a refreshing and tangy scent. Ribbons, beads and several undecorated fruit complete the arrangement.

❧ VETIVER BELL
Made of vetiver,
which has a persistent,
sweet aroma, this bell is
filled with a beautiful display
of dried plant materials,
including achillea, fir cones, roses,
Doronicum and mosses. The
nutmeg and cinnamon sticks relate
the design to the kitchen and the warm
colors ensure the arrangement is eye-catching.

ꞏ NATURAL STORES ꞏ

KITCHEN DECORATIONS can range from the incredibly simple to the very complicated with infinite variations in between. Decorations need not be traditional; indeed you can be as innovative as you wish. However, when creating a display for the kitchen, remember to include some elements in your design that are related to cooking or food and be sure not to overestimate the available space. Small kitchens are easily overwhelmed with the everyday clutter of cooking, so if your kitchen is tiny make small and simple decorations that will brighten dark corners. For a sizable kitchen, you can be more adventurous and create a large, imposing arrangement. As with the size of the design, the strength of the perfume should vary in accordance with the size of the kitchen. A large, old-fashioned or drafty kitchen will require a stronger perfume than a small, modern kitchen.

❀ CORN SACK
Filled with cloves and decorated with wheat ears and cinnamon sticks, this tiny sack exudes a spicy fragrance.

❀ SCENTED STORE
This wooden frame contains fragrant herb and spice mixes as well as flowers, in a formal design. The delicious scent of the potpourri seeps through the wood.

NUTMEG

ORANGE PEEL　　　　ROSEMARY　　　　CLOVES　　　　CARDAMOMS

❀ BRASS BOWL *Originally used for skimming cream, this bowl displays the sharp, citrus-yellows of the mix to perfection. A vibrant contrast is provided by the violet-blue mallows. The perfumes of lemon balm and rosemary pervade this mix.*

❀ SLIPWARE DISH *In this potpourri, spices, flowers, herbs, seedpods, seedheads and citrus peel combine to produce an interesting texture as well as to provide a brightly colored display and a delicious perfume of citrus and marigold.*

CINNAMON STICK

DORONICUM

MARSH MARIGOLD

SENNA PODS

SCABIOUS

EVERLASTING FLOWERS

COCKSCOMB

ACHILLEA

MALLOW

ORANGE PEEL

EVERLASTING FLOWERS

OAKMOSS

GRASS SEEDHEADS

POTENTILLA

STAR ANISE

POTENTILLA

❧ POTPOURRIS ❧

Potpourris for the kitchen should have a strong, fruity, herby or spicy scent to cut through the cooking smells, so often prevalent there, without clashing with them. Use food containers, such as jelly molds, platters, dinner plates and bowls, and oven dishes to emphasize further the relationship between the potpourri and the kitchen. For a subtle effect, decorate the mixes with plant material of complementary colors; for a more vivid display use flowers of contrasting colors. You can achieve a most interesting effect by decorating a mixture with plant material specifically used in the kitchen – seeds, herbs and spices are all suitable. Stand the completed arrangements on the table, dresser or windowsill, or try putting one in a hanging basket and suspending it from a beam. Avoid placing potpourris on busy work surfaces, where they may be in the way, or close to the cooker and its accompanying steam, which will cause the scent to deteriorate quickly.

❀ SCARLET BASKET *This rich blue potpourri contrasts strongly with the scarlet basket. Coriander adds a spicy touch to the herb-scented mix.*

LARKSPUR

LAVENDER

CINNAMON STICKS

❧ BURNING PERFUME ❧

CANDLES IN THE KITCHEN evoke a nostalgic, rustic atmosphere. Eating by their mellow light transforms any meal into a special occasion, and the atmosphere is made more memorable if the candles are scented. Candles in the kitchen can be perfumed with herbs, oils and essences, or perhaps the unique, honeyed fragrance of beeswax is the most appealing. Single candles are lovely displayed in traditional holders or on saucers, although table candelabras, holding several tapering candles, will provide more light. An intriguing mixture of perfumes is produced by grouping an assortment of tiny, fragrant candles on a plate. Night lights can be placed in a perfume vaporizer where they will produce a muted light and a strong scent as the perfume evaporates.

❀ MATCHING HERB CANDLES
These candles are all decorated with old-fashioned, cottage-garden herbs. They are scented with lemon balm, thyme, rosemary and bergamot.

❀ HEART-SHAPED CANDLE
This peppermint-scented candle (left) is decorated with borage.

❀ DAINTY CANDLES
Tiny, decorated candles (left) are very effective when clustered on a plate.

❀ **BAYBERRY CANDLES** *These simple and pleasing candles are scented with bayberry essence.*

❀ **BEESWAX CANDLES** *The rich, honeyed scent of these candles adds to their charm.*

❀ **PERFUME VAPORIZER** *The bowl of perfume is placed above the lighted candle and the heat from the candle causes the perfume to evaporate, so creating a pervading aroma.*

❧ RECIPES ❧

POTPOURRIS FOR DISPLAY

SPICY LEMON MIX

2pt (1 liter) MIXED BLUE FLOWERS
1oz (30g) ORRIS ROOT
POWDER
1 FINELY CRUSHED
CINNAMON STICK
2 TEASPOONS ALLSPICE
BERRIES
4 DROPS CLOVE OIL
4 DROPS GERANIUM OIL
4 DROPS LEMON OIL

*The **Scented Store** (pp.48-49) is filled with this dry potpourri. Three of the compartments contain potpourri, decorated with blue flowers. To add to the bouquet of the potpourri the other compartments are filled with lavender, rosemary, nutmegs, cardamoms, cloves, citrus peel, fir cones and oakmoss. When putting the potpourri in the compartments, be sure to cover it with pretty flowers. This is for decoration and also because it contains orris root powder, which will cloud the glass if it comes in direct contact with it. Hang the picture in a warm place so that the scent is stronger.*

❀ PESTLE
& MORTAR
Fresh, crushed herbs fill the kitchen with a lovely aroma.

HERB & SPICE MIX

2pt (1 liter) BLUE LARKSPUR
FLOWERS
2oz (60g) MIXED SWEET HERBS
1oz (30g) FINE-GROUND
GUM BENZOIN
2 TEASPOONS CARAWAY SEEDS
1 TEASPOON CORIANDER SEEDS
PEEL OF A LEMON
4 DROPS CORIANDER OIL
2 DROPS LEMON OIL
LITTLE BUNDLE OF CINNAMON
STICKS, LAVENDER &
LARKSPUR SPIKES TO
DECORATE

*The **Scarlet Basket** (p.51) is filled with this dry potpourri in which fragrant herbs and spices are carefully blended to produce a subtle bouquet.*

CITRUS & MARIGOLD MIX

1pt (500ml) MIXED YELLOW
& ORANGE FLOWERS
1pt (500ml) LEMON VERBENA
1oz (30g) MIXED SWEET HERBS
1oz (30g) OAKMOSS
1oz (30g) SENNA PODS
1oz (30g) ORRIS ROOT POWDER
2 TEASPOONS CINNAMON POWDER
2 BROKEN CINNAMON STICKS
PEEL OF 1/2 AN ORANGE
PEEL OF 1/2 A LEMON
4 DROPS MARIGOLD OIL
2 DROPS ORANGE OIL
1 DROP LEMON OIL
YELLOW DORONICUM FLOWERS
& SEEDHEADS TO DECORATE

*The **Slipware Dish** (pp.50-51) contains this dry potpourri. The ingredients blend to produce a beautiful display as well as a captivating perfume.*

SPICE MIX

1pt (500ml) MIXED WHOLE
SPICES – SUCH AS ALLSPICE
BERRIES, CARDAMOMS
CINNAMON STICKS,
CLOVES, CORIANDER SEEDS,
JUNIPER BERRIES,
NUTMEGS & STAR ANISE
1pt (500ml) MIXED SEEDHEADS
– SUCH AS AQUILEGIA, CLEMATIS,
HELLEBORE, LOVE-IN-A-MIST, POPPY,
QUEEN-ANNE'S-LACE & WHEAT EARS
1oz (30g) LAVENDER
1oz (30g) FINE-GROUND
GUM BENZOIN
4 DROPS VETIVER OIL
2 DROPS LAVENDER OIL
2 DROPS LEMON OIL

This beautifully textured and brightly colored dry potpourri is ideal for displaying in the kitchen.

GERANIUM & LEMON MIX

1pt (500ml) BLUE LARKSPUR
FLOWERS
1pt (500ml) LEMON VERBENA
2oz (60g) LAVENDER
1oz (30g) FINE-GROUND
GUM BENZOIN
1 TEASPOON CARAWAY SEEDS
1 TEASPOON
CORIANDER SEEDS
1 TEASPOON CLOVES
4 DROPS GERANIUM OIL
2 DROPS LEMON OIL

The geranium oil in this dry potpourri produces quite a musky perfume, which is sharpened by the lemon verbena and spices. The color mixture of blue and green is lovely in the kitchen.

❀ HERBS & POMANDERS *The bright colors and invigorating aromas of a bunch of herbs (below) and a tangy pomander (above right) are delightful in the kitchen.*

LEMON & ROSEMARY MIX

2pt (1 liter) MIXED YELLOW FLOWERS
2oz (60g) LEMON BALM LEAVES
1oz (30g) ROSEMARY
1oz (30g) ORRIS ROOT POWDER
2 TEASPOONS ALLSPICE BERRIES
1 TEASPOON CUMIN SEEDS
PEEL OF A LEMON
4 DROPS MELISSA
(LEMON BALM) OIL
2 DROPS ROSEMARY OIL
BLUE FLOWERS TO DECORATE

*The **Brass Bowl** (p.50) displays this brightly colored dry potpourri. It is wonderful in the kitchen as its overall scent is lemony.*

CITRUS PEEL MIX

2pt (1 liter) MIXED CITRUS PEEL
1oz (30g) MARIGOLD FLOWERS
1oz (30g) ROSEMARY
1oz (30g) FINE-GROUND
GUM BENZOIN
2 DROPS LEMON OIL
2 DROPS MARIGOLD OIL
2 DROPS ORANGE OIL
2 DROPS TANGERINE OIL

This dry potpourri is a lovely blend of tangy citrus fruit and heady marigold.

BURNING PERFUME

MUSKY ORANGE

10 DROPS ORANGE OIL
2 DROPS FRANKINCENSE OIL

*The **Perfume Vaporizer** (p.53) is burning this deliciously scented mix. Pretty ceramic vaporizers are available from many gift shops. Small nightlights are used to vaporize the perfume in the saucer, which is placed over the light. The nightlight need only be burnt for 5 minutes or so as the perfume will continue to vaporize after the light is turned off. Experiment with different fragrant oils to discover your favorites.*

SCENTED CANDLES

With practice scented candles can be made at home. However, I advise reading a book on the subject before starting. Be careful, as wax is highly flammable.

Make scented candles by infusing sprigs of dried or fresh herbs in wax heated in a double saucepan to 46.5°F (82°C) for about half an hour. Remove the herbs and make the candles either by using molds or by dipping. Chopped fresh or dried herbs can be scattered through the candle for decoration.

PERFUMING WAX

12oz (360g) WAX
6 DROPS CANDLE PERFUME

Slowly add perfume to the melted wax so that it distributes evenly throughout. Special candle perfumes are best but essential oils can be used. Make the candles by using molds or by dipping.

COLORING CANDLES

WAX CRAYONS OR SPECIAL WAX
COLORING DISCS

***Bayberry Candles** (p.53). Slowly add coloring to the melted wax. Add bayberry essence and make the candles as above.*

THE DINING ROOM

WHETHER YOU HAVE a dining room that is elegant and sophisticated or informal country-style, you can perfume it in many delightful ways. Like the banqueting halls of ages past, you can strew the floors with sweet-smelling herbs, although the concept might prove a little overwhelming in the smaller rooms of this day and age! A better idea may be to re-create the potpourris of our ancestors by gathering the same materials from the garden as they did, mixing them with spices and finally adding the precious essential oils. Make sure that the fragrance is not too strong, so that the appetizing aromas of the food can be savored. The soft and gentle perfumes of lavender, roses, heliotrope, geranium and lemon verbena are perfect as they remain in the background and only manifest their fragrance when there

❁ SCENTED LINEN *Napkins (above) and tablecloths are imbued with gentle fragrances by storing them with scented sachets in a linen press (left) or dresser.*

is no other to compete with. Create pretty, perfumed sachets and cushions that reflect the colors of your dining room or an intricate and sumptuous table centerpiece. Look for inspiration for designs in decorative china, embroidery and even fragile lace doilies. Make the most of the subtle colors and fascinating textures of dried botanicals. Arrange tiny bouquets to adorn napkin rings or place settings or large displays to loop over chair backs, all redolent with gentle perfumes. Design deep-framed collages using a variety of potpourris and scented botanicals, arranged in geometic or abstract designs. The different perfumes will gradually seep through the back of the frame and gently scent the room. To celebrate a special occasion, burn fragrant candles. They are simple to make and can be decorated with herbs and flowers.

POTPOURRIS

THE DINING-ROOM TABLE is the ideal surface for displaying a large potpourri as a center-piece. Add small, matching posies to each place setting to complete the overall look. Make sure that the scent is not so overwhelming that it impairs your enjoyment of the food – light, floral or tangy fragrances are ideal.

❊ SMALL BOWL
In this informally arranged potpourri, the traditional scent of lavender and roses is sharpened by the addition of orange peel.

STAR ANISE

ROSES

LAVENDER

BLUEBELLS   AZALEA

ACHILLEA

BLUE LARKSPUR

WHITE LARKSPUR

COLOMBINE

CLOVES   FLAME-OF-THE-FOREST

GLOBE AMARANTH

QUEEN-ANNE'S-LACE

ROSE BUD

MOCK ORANGE BLOSSOM

WATER FORGET-ME-NOT

CINNAMON STICK

OAKMOSS

❊ WHITE DISH *The formal appearance of this potpourri is accentuated by the lines of cinnamon sticks. A sweet and tangy scent of bergamot orange is softened by a hint of lavender.*

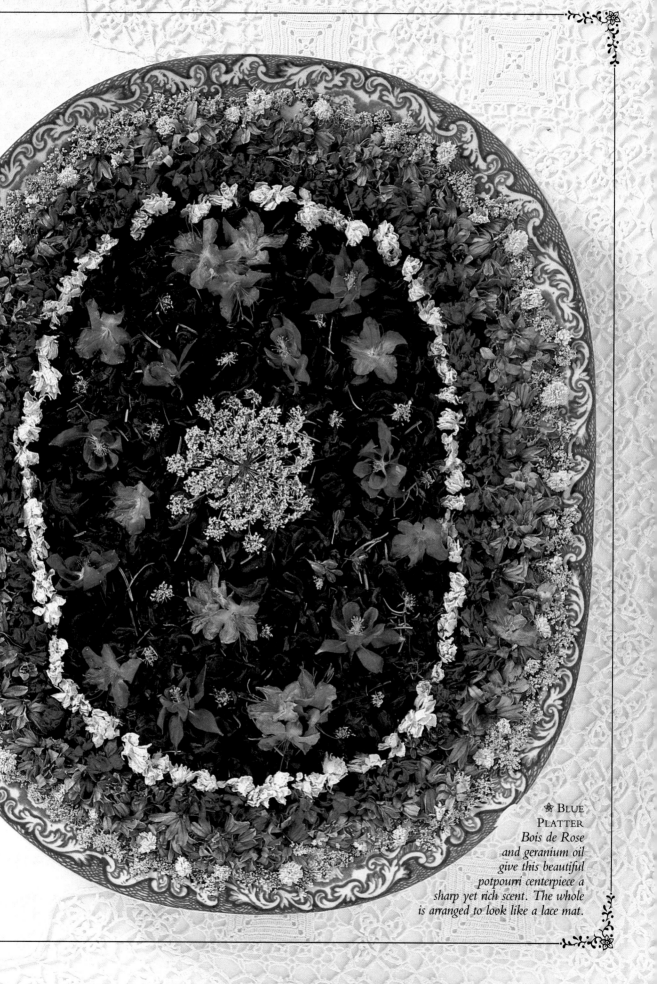

❀ BLUE
PLATTER
*Bois de Rose
and geranium oil
give this beautiful
potpourri centerpiece a
sharp yet rich scent. The whole
is arranged to look like a lace mat.*

✿ RED WINE *Wine has
a pleasing bouquet,
which adds to the ambience
of an evening meal.*

✿ POPPYSEED ROLL
*Fresh bread has a
wonderfully
appetizing aroma.*

TABLE DECOR

SCENTED DECORATIONS for the dining-room table make an important dinner party or romantic evening meal even more special. Matching posies for each place setting are very effective. Alternatively, if you feel adventurous, a floral centerpiece of dried flowers looks stunning. If you also perfume the napkins and tablecloth, ensure that the fragrance of the floral decorations complements them.

❀ FLORAL CENTERPIECE
Beautifully made with rose buds, roses, globe amaranths, Queen-Anne's-lace and larkspur, this flower-scented decoration (above) looks perfect placed in the center of the dining table.

❀ LILAC NAPKIN
Store delicately scented sachets with napkins and tablecloths to imbue them with a gentle perfume.

AROMATIC FOOD

THERE ARE many plant materials that can be used to enhance the appearance, flavor and fragrance of food. Herbs and spices are renowned for their flavorsome properties; less well known is that flower petals and leaves can be used in a similar way. The lovely shapes and colors of flowers make them ideal for decorating sweet dishes and their scent adds a delicate flavor. Try making everyday foods, such as butter and sugar, more exciting by garnishing and flavoring them with flowers, and decorate cakes and chocolates with crystallized flowers.

❀ ROSE-PETAL JAM
Rose-petal jam is delicately flavored and has a gentle, delicate perfume.

❀ FLORAL CHOCOLATES
Mint chocolates decorated with crystallized flowers are a lovely gift.

❀ FLOWER BUTTER
Violets, lavender and sweet cicely leaves decorate this butter.

❀ SCENTED SUGAR
Store a vanilla pod and lavender with sugar to make a scented sweetener.

❀ ELDER FLOWER CHAMPAGNE *Elder flowers make a wonderful, fragrant, fizzy champagne.*

❀ FLOWER CAKE
This beautiful moist sponge cake is decorated with crystallized flowers for a teatime treat.

❧ CUSHIONS & SACHETS ❧

Filled with potpourri or a herbal mix, cushions and sachets are perfect decorations for the dining room. For seat cushions, make sure that the scent of the filling is not too powerful as you will need to use a sizable amount. By contrast, sachets are so small that the mix used for them should be quite strongly scented or it will be lost.

Place cushions on chair seats and suspend sachets from the backs. The possibilites for displaying sachets are endless: loop them on the drawer handles of the dresser; hang them over the radiators; or place them in the drawers of the sideboard to scent napkins and tablecloths. Cushions and sachets look especially effective if they match one another. Little dried-flower bouquets or embroidered flowers are excellent as finishing touches of decoration.

✿ CHAIR SACHETS
Filled with a rose and geranium mix, these charming bags are lovely decorations for chair arms and backs.

✿ CHAIR CUSHIONS
To make a cushion that is comfortable as well as sweet-smelling, place the scented mix in an envelope of wadding and insert the whole into a cushion cover.

❈ RED STYLE
*Lavender and
lemon verbena
fill this bag,
which is ideal for
looping on a
door handle.*

❈ SILK HEARTS
*Small, silk roses
decorate these little,
silk taffeta sachets,
which have been
filled with rose
petals.*

❈ REGENCY
ELEGANCE
*A bergamot
and lavender
mix fills these
tiny Regency
silk sachets.*

❈ FLOWER GARDEN
*This heliotrope-scented,
Victorian ribbon sachet
is decorated with a
pressed-flower collage.*

❧ FRAMED SCENT ❧

IN MANY HOUSEHOLDS most meals are eaten in the kitchen; the dining room is reserved for special occasions. If you tend to use your dining room infrequently, make sure that the scented decorations you create for it are long-lasting as well as beautiful. Arrangements under glass are ideal as they retain their scent and color for much longer than a design that is open to the air. The scent escapes slowly through the back of the picture ensuring that it will never overpower the aroma of the food. Use different potpourris to construct an abstract design, such as the fan shown on this page, or create a still life. Always decorate the potpourri with whole flowers so that the powdery mix does not come into contact with the glass. Three-dimensional pictures can be displayed flat on the dresser or table or hung on the wall. If you are a handy carpenter you could make a beautiful and unique table by attaching legs to the underside of the frame and covering the potpourri collage with strong glass.

❀ THREE-DIMENSIONAL FAN *This wooden frame is filled with potpourri and a variety of scented botanicals to create a beautiful, fan-shaped and highly perfumed arrangement.*

SANDALWOOD

ROSE

LEMON VERBENA

FIR CONES

LARKSPUR

NUTMEG

CINNAMON STICKS

LAVENDER

CLOVES

GLOBE AMARANTH

FLAME-OF-THE-FOREST

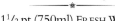

ROSE-PETAL JAM

❊

1¹/₂ pt (750ml) Fresh Water
1lb (500g) Granulated Sugar
8oz (250g) Rose Petals
Juice of 2 Lemons

***Rose Petal Jam** (p.62)*. Bruise the petals,
discarding the white heals. Put them in a
bowl, sprinkle with half the sugar and leave
overnight. Dissolve the remaining sugar in
a pan with the lemon juice and water. Add
the rose and sugar mixture and simmer for
20 minutes. Increase heat and boil for about 5
minutes until thick. Pour in jars and seal.

POTPOURRIS FOR CUSHIONS

REGENCY MIX

❊

1pt (500ml) Red Roses
1pt (500ml) Mixed Cassia Bark
& Sandalwood Shavings
2oz (60g) Lavender
1oz (30g) Orris Root Powder
1oz (30g) Cloves
2 Teaspoons Cinnamon Powder
4 Drops Rose Oil
2 Drops Clary Sage Oil
2 Drops Sandalwood Oil

*The **Chair Cushions** (p.64) are filled
with this intriguing dry potpourri.*

ELDERFLOWER CHAMPAGNE

*Elderflowers impart a distinctive flavor
like that of the Muscat grape.*

8pt (4 liters) Fresh Water
1¹/₂lb (750g) Granulated Sugar
6 Medium Flowerheads of Elder
2 Tablespoons White Wine Vinegar
2 Lemons

***Elderflower Champagne** (pp.62-63)*.
Sterilize all the equipment. Dissolve
the sugar in a little of the water.
Squeeze juice from the lemons and
cut the rind into strips. Put washed
flowers in a large non-metallic
container with the lemon juice
and rind, sugar-water,
vinegar and remaining
water. Stir and cover.
Leave for 5 days.
Strain liquid and pour
into screw-top bottles.
Serve chilled.

❧ RECIPES ❧

AROMATIC FOOD & DRINK

When gathering flowers for use in cooking
make sure they are edible. Pick them
when they are dry and newly opened
and be sure that they are clean
and free from insects.

CRYSTALLIZED FLOWERS & LEAVES

❊

Selection of Edible
Flowers & Leaves
Lightly Whisked Egg White
Superfine Sugar

*To decorate **Floral Chocolates** and
Flower Cake (pp.62-63)*. Brush egg
white over the flowers and leaves. Lightly
dredge with sugar. Place them on greaseproof
paper on a baking sheet and dry in a very
cool oven, with the door ajar, for 3 hours.
Use as decoration, securing them
in place with beaten egg white.

❊ Finger Bowl
*A slice of lemon in
warm water makes
a lovely rinse for hands.*

POTPOURRIS FOR DISPLAY

TANGY MIX

1pt (500ml) Mixed White
or Cream Flowers
1pt (500ml) Lavender
2oz (60g) Oakmoss
1oz (30g) Orris Root Powder
1 Teaspoon Crushed
Cardamom Seeds
3 Tonka Beans
4 Drops Bergamot Oil
2 Drops Lavender Oil
Water Forget-me-nots
& Cream Roses to Decorate

*The **White Dish** (p.58) displays
this tangy dry potpourri.*

RICH ROSE MIX

2pt (1 liter) Roses & Rose Petals
2oz (60g) Mixed Sweet Herbs
1oz (30g) Fine-ground Gum Benzoin
2 Teaspoons Cinnamon Powder
1 Teaspoon Cloves
1 Star Anise
Peel of an Orange
4 Drops Rose Oil
2 Drops Lavender Oil
Whole Roses to Decorate

*The **Small Bowl** (p.58) is filled with this
dry rose potpourri, a traditional mix.*

BLUE & WHITE MIX

1pt (500ml) Flame-of-the-Forest
1pt (500ml) Mixed Pale Blue
& White Flowers
2oz (60g) Rosemary
(1oz) 30g Lavender
1oz (30g) Orris Root Powder
2 Teaspoons Cinnamon Powder
1/2 Teaspoon Coriander Seeds
4 Drops Bois de Rose Oil
2 Drops Geranium Oil
Queen-Anne's-lace, Blue Columbines
& Blue Azaleas to Decorate

*The **Blue Platter** (p.59) is decorated with
this elegant blue and white dry potpourri.*

TRADITIONAL ROSE MIX

1pt (500ml) Mixed Whole Roses
& Rose Petals
1pt (500ml) Mixed Calamus
& Woodruff Leaves
1oz (30g) Orris Root Powder
4 Crushed Tonka Beans
2 Chopped Vanilla Pods
2 Teaspoons Allspice
2 Teaspoons Crushed Musk Seeds
2 Teaspoons Crushed Mace
4 Drops Clary Sage Oil
4 Drops Rose Oil
2 Drops Bergamot Oil
Whole Roses to Decorate

*The large middle compartment of the **Three-
dimensional Fan** (pp.66-67) is filled with
this musky dry potpourri.*

POTPOURRIS FOR SACHETS

HELIOTROPE MIX

2pt (1 liter) Heliotrope Flowers
or Rose Petals
2oz (60g) Orris Root Powder
4 Ground Tonka Beans
2 Chopped Vanilla Pods
6 Drops Heliotrope Oil

*The **Flower Garden Sachet** (p.65) is
filled with this sweet-scented dry potpourri.
Try using 4 drops of rose oil,
4 drops of neroli oil, 2 chopped vanilla
pods and 2 drops of almond essence
instead of the heliotrope oil.*

ROSE, PATCHOULI & GERANIUM MIX

1pt (500ml) Scented Geranium
(Pelargonium) Leaves
1pt (500ml) Dry, Fragrant Sawdust
2oz (60g) Lavender
1oz (30g) Orris Root Powder
1 Teaspoon Cloves
4 Drops Geranium Oil
4 Drops Rose Oil
2 Drops Patchouli Oil

*The **Chair Sachets** (p.64) are filled
with this rich, evocative dry potpourri.*

✽ CANDLE *Tiny
scented candles
are delightful in
the dining room.*

TRADITIONAL ROSE-PETAL MOIST MIX

2pt (1 liter) Crumbled
Stock-pot Petals
2oz (60g) Lavender
2oz (60g) Chopped Angelica
and/or Eryngium Root
1oz (30g) Orris Root Powder
Peel of 1/2 an Orange
1 Teaspoon Cloves
4 Drops Rose Oil
2 Drops Lavender Oil
2 Drops Geranium,
Spikenard or Sumbul Oil

*The **Silk Hearts** (p.65) are filled
with this rosy moist potpourri.*

BERGAMOT MIX

1pt (500ml) Bergamot Leaves
& Flowers
1pt (500ml) Mixed Calamus,
Melilot and/
or Sweet Vernal
Grass & Woodruff
1oz (30g) Lavender
1oz (30g) Orris Root Powder
2 Tonka Beans
1 Teaspoon Allspice
4 Drops Monarda Oil
2 Drops Angelica Oil
2 Drops Geranium Oil

*The **Regency Elegance Sachets**
(p.65) are filled with this sharp,
musky dry potpourri.*

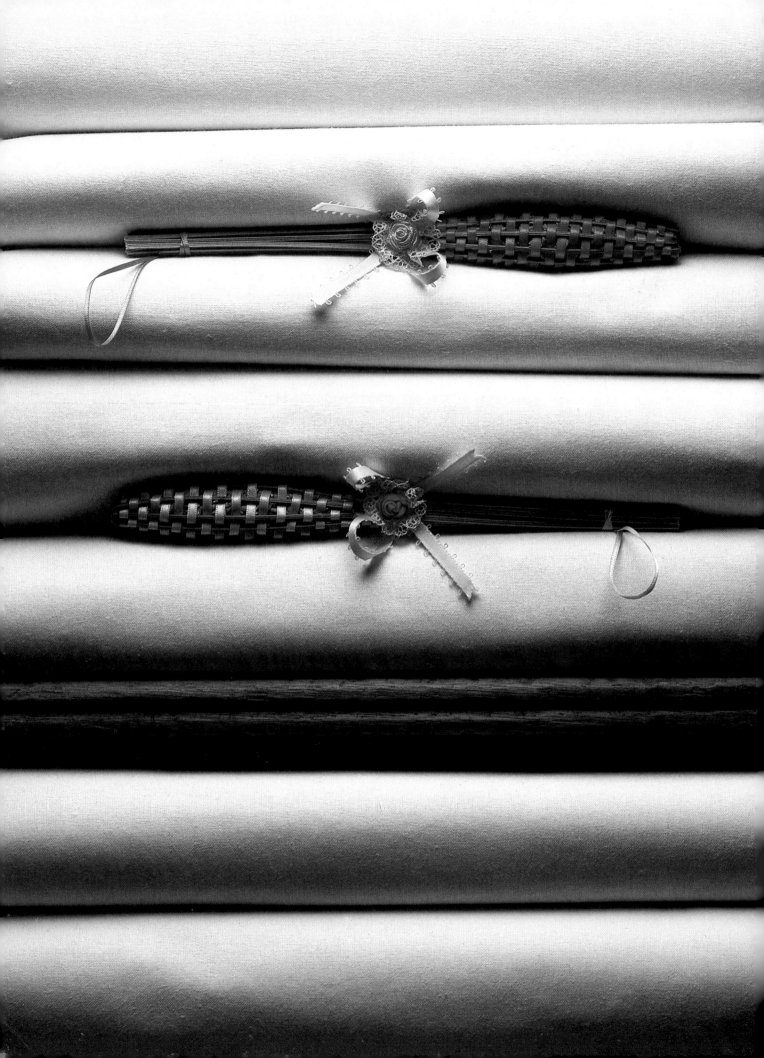

THE BEDROOM

WHATEVER THE STYLE of your bedroom – intimate and Victorian, stark and modern, or traditional and chintzy – you can make it redolent with complementary perfumes. An ideal potpourri for the bedroom is the lovely rose, lavender and carnation mix, which you can sharpen by adding peppermint, orange or lemon. Fill pillows with soothing potpourris. Try stuffing a large pillow with a hop, lemon and lavender mix – recommended by George III as an excellent sleep inducer. Another traditional filler for pillows is a mixture of

❀ SCENTED DELIGHTS *The exquisite lavender bundles (left) and the delicate sachets (above) are ideal for scenting clothes and linen.*

woodruff and agrimony leaves. The coumarin contained in them becomes more fragrant with age. Old, white lacy pillows, cushions and nightdress cases, beloved of the Victorians, look delightful in almost any bedroom, as do little antique lace sachets, although you can use any fabric

you like. Fill sachets with much stronger mixes than pillows. Make these soft and floral, hot and spicy, herby or even camphorous. Pop little moth-repellant sachets in drawers and hang them in wardrobes. Drawer liners can also be scented with a moth-repellant mix, or you can try a floral one if you prefer. Floral pomanders are lovely and a little unusual, or try making simple citrus pomanders – often men prefer the hot fragrance. Unglazed lidded pots will diffuse perfume into the room. Just drop a little essential oil into the pot before filling it with a very strong potpourri – marigold is an excellent fragrance to use. Place the pots by the bedside so that the soothing perfume drifts over you as you sleep. Store natural beauty products in old bottles or jars. Arranged on the dressing table they are both useful and decorative.

❀ NIGHTDRESS CASE
(below) Place a scented sachet, filled with a favorite mix, in your nightdress case.

❀ SCATTER CUSHIONS
Scented with a gentle and soothing potpourri, these lovely lacy pillows (above and below) produce a beautiful subtle fragrance and are an attractive decoration for the bedroom.

❧ SATIN & WHITE LACE ❧

PILLOWS FOR THE BEDROOM can be filled with soothing herbal mixes or light, floral potpourris. Arranged on the bed, they will perfume the whole room as well as scent the bedlinen. Try filling the pillows with a mix containing hops – traditionally held to be a relaxant – and the gentle fragrance will help you to sleep. White pillow cases embroidered or covered with lace look lovely in any bedroom as their traditional designs complement most decorations. If you prefer to have patterned pillowcases, use muted colors to complement relaxing fragrances, and bright colors to accentuate more pervasive perfumes.

❀ SLEEP PILLOW
Filled with a soothing mix, largely of hops but with a hint of lavender, this pillow is beneficial for all those who have trouble sleeping.

POMANDERS & SACHETS

SCENTED DECORATIONS that can be suspended are useful for the bedroom where flat surfaces may be limited to the bedside table and the dressing table. Hang floral pomanders in eye-catching positions – from the curtain rod perhaps, or over the dressing-table mirror. Place citrus pomanders in similar positions or hang them in the closet where they will transfer their lovely tangy scent to your clothes. Pretty cloth sachets are perfect for looping over door handles, drawer knobs, radiators or any suitable hook. Pastel shades are very often best for the bedroom. However, a wonderful way to make a stunning impact in a simply decorated bedroom is to create sachets and pomanders in bold colors.

❀ CITRUS & LACE *A tangy, orange pomander surrounded by lacy netting can be put on show in the bedroom.*

❀ BLUE & WHITE HEARTS *Hang this elegant, camphor- and lavender-scented sachet chain in front of a window or beside the dressing table for a lovely effect.*

❀ RIBBON SACHETS *These two scented sachets match the floral pomanders opposite in both fragrance and appearance. They are lovely grouped together.*

❀ RIBBON & LACE
*This beautiful sachet
is filled with a mixed
floral potpourri and
would look beautiful
hanging in front of
dark curtains
or furniture.*

❀ LAVENDER–BLUE
POMANDER *Made
from lavender
flowers and blue
floral ribbon,
this pomander
is scented with
lavender and cloves.*

❀ ROSE–RED POMANDER
*Decorated with a variety
of bright pink and red
flowers, this pretty
rose-scented, floral
pomander is truly
eye-catching.*

CREAMS, FLORAL WATERS & COLOGNES

PERFUMES AND COSMETICS are simple to make at home and, as well as being very natural, they are a wonderful addition to the scent and decoration of the bedroom. Flowers, herbs and essential oils are used to perfume home-made cosmetics. The scent you choose is a matter of personal preference, although some plants, such as elder flowers and chamomile, are particularly suitable for making creams and oils as they possess soothing and cleansing properties. Choose attractive bottles, jars and pots for your cosmetics, and decorate them with ribbons and pressed flowers.

❀ HONEYSUCKLE CREAM *This deliciously fragrant honeysuckle cream (right) is perfect for soothing areas of dry skin and for use as a body lotion.*

❀ JONQUILS *Fresh, highly scented jonquils are lovely in the bedroom.*

❀ ELDER FLOWER CREAM *Elder flower cream (left) has a refreshing fragrance and can be used as a nourishing and toning cream for the face and body.*

❀ FLORAL COLOGNES
Sweet-scented flowers can be used to produce lovely colognes. These bottles (far left) contain jonquil cologne (see p.120) and violet and heliotrope cologne.

❀ ROSE WATER & BODY OIL
The dark blue bottle (far right) contains rose water – a sweet-scented perfume. Body oil (right), made with almond oil and any essential oil, (see p.120) is perfect for softening the skin.

❀ FRAGRANT TALCUM POWDER
A few drops of a favorite essential oil transforms unscented talc into something special.

❀ HAND CREAM *This hand cream is scented with a few drops of essential oil.*

❧ POTPOURRIS ❧

PRETTY AND DELICATE floral potpourris are popular for the bedroom, as they lend themselves well to the soothing, pastel colors in which many bedrooms are decorated. However, if your bedroom is filled with primary colors and bold abstracts, then be daring and create a potpourri that is as vibrant as its surroundings. A formally decorated potpourri looks wonderful in a bedroom full of stripes and geometric shapes, while informal designs are more suited to a floral decor. Display the potpourri on the dressing table or make matching mixes for each bedside table. Do not make the scent so strong that your sleep is disturbed and, if you have made herb pillows for the bed, ensure that the perfume of your mix complements that of the pillows.

STATICE

ROSE

POTENTILLA

LAVENDER

GLOBE AMARANTH

❀ SHALLOW DISH
The pattern of this vibrant pink potpourri (above) is just like a formal flower border. The musky carnation scent is lifted by tangy orange.

ROSES

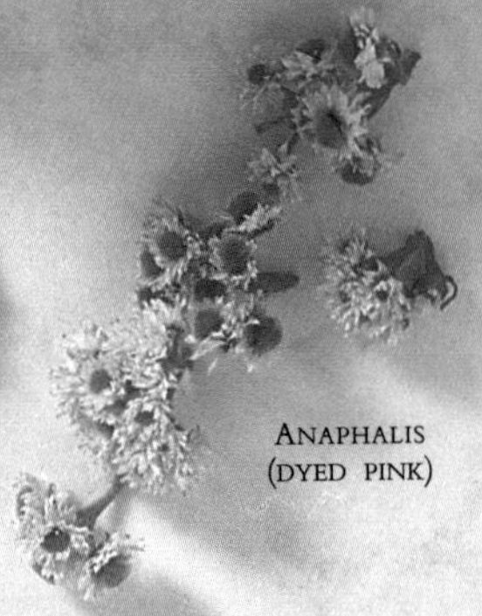

ANAPHALIS (DYED PINK)

BLUEBELLS

✤ NAUTILUS SHELL
*The moist potpourri inside
this polished nautilus shell
is decorated with rose buds
and bluebells, so that its
soothing, traditional scent
of rose and lavender
escapes slowly.*

ROSE BUDS

ROSES

FLAME-OF-THE-
FOREST

DEUTZIA

POTENTILLA

BLUEBELLS

✤ SMALL SILVER
BOWL *Peppermint oil
gently sharpens the
overall floral perfume of
this dark blue potpourri
(right), which is
decorated with roses,
deutzia blossoms
and bluebells.*

POLYGONUM
CAMPANULATUM

ROSES

❧ CERAMIC STYLES ❧

SMALL, SELF-CONTAINED SCENTED DECORATIONS are ideal for the bedroom, especially if space is limited. Ornamental, unglazed ceramic pots make excellent containers for potpourris or essential oils. The scent of the mixture is absorbed by the unglazed pottery and exudes slowly into the room, allowing the use of a strong perfume that might otherwise be too overpowering for the bedroom. Decorative, unglazed ceramic shapes, such as the hearts below, are useful for placing in odd corners, for scenting jewelry boxes, wardrobes and chests of drawers, and for making a display on the dressing table or the bedside table. Perfume the shapes by soaking them in a fragrant essence or essential oil. Other small and attractive items, such as shells, are also suitable for displaying in the bedroom and are easily scented in the same way, or by putting a few drops of an essential oil or potpourri reviver in their centers. If you enjoy strong, heady perfumes, try burning one or two joss sticks. Make sure that you like the perfume before you light them as the scent tends to be very persistent.

❀ LARGE DECORATIVE TERRACOTTA JAR *This attractive blue, red and white jar is filled with a richly fragrant, mixed-flower potpourri that complements its colors.*

❀ BLUE HEARTS *Several, small pottery hearts, scented with lavender essence or an essential oil, make a simple decoration.*

❈ MATCHING
TERRACOTTA JARS
*Filled with a lightly
scented rose, lavender
and peppermint pot-
pourri, these jars are
ideal for displaying
on the bedside table.*

❈ SHELLS *The shapes of
seashells make them
naturally decorative.
They are scented
with a rose
perfume.*

STAR TURBAN

TURBAN SHELL

STRIPED TOP

❈ JOSS STICKS
*These simple room
perfumers from the
East can be used to
create a mysterious,
hazy atmosphere
in the bedroom.*

COMMERCIAL TROCHUS

↭ SACHETS & DRAWER LINERS ↭

FILL YOUR BEDROOM WITH SCENT by placing pretty, perfumed sachets in all available nooks and crannies. Sachets contain only a small amount of potpourri, so long-lasting and strong fragrances are recommended. Try to maintain an overall blending of perfume, and use fragrances that are suitable for scenting your clothes, the bedlinen and the room. Men often prefer spicy aromas. A combination of bergamot, orange and rosemary is very effective, and rose, caraway, thyme and cloves also produce a popular masculine scent. Protect your clothes from insects by scenting drawer liners with tansy, wormwood and rosemary.

❀ HEARTS & LACE
Delicate little sachets like these (above and below) are ideal for scenting lingerie.

❀ EMBROIDERED SQUARES *Ideal for a handkerchief drawer, these sachets (below) exude the old-fashioned fragrances of camphor and lavender.*

❀ NEEDLEWORK CUSHION *Decorate your bedroom chair with a pretty cushion filled with a soothing potpourri.*

❀ FRESH BLUE
These sachets contain a sweet flag potpourri, which has a scent of violets with spicy overtones.

❋ DRAWER LINERS
*Line your drawers
with perfumed paper
to ensure that your
clothes are always
sweetly scented.*

❋ DAINTY LACE
*Round or square,
lace sachets are
perfect for placing
among clothes
and bedlinen.*

❧ RECIPES ❧

FOR THE BODY

ROSE WATER

❋

1/2pt (250ml) VODKA
10 DROPS ROSE OIL

Rose Water (p.77). Add rose oil to vodka. Shake well. Bottle and cork.

VIOLET & HELIOTROPE COLOGNE

❋

4oz (120g) ORRIS ROOT
1/2pt (250ml) VODKA
4 DROPS HELIOTROPE OIL

Violet & Heliotrope Cologne (p.77). Put orris root and vodka in a lidded jar. Infuse for 10 days, shaking daily. Strain and add heliotrope oil. Shake well. Bottle and cork.

ELDERFLOWER CREAM

❋

6fl oz (180ml) ALMOND OIL
1 TABLESPOON LANOLIN
1 CUP ELDERFLOWERS

Elderflower Cream (p.76). Melt lanolin in a bowl placed in a pan of hot water. Mix in almond oil. Add elderflowers. Heat in a pan of simmering water for 30 minutes. Strain and cool. Pack in a lidded jar.

HONEYSUCKLE CREAM

❋

4oz (120g) PETROLEUM JELLY
1oz (30g) FRESH HONEYSUCKLE BLOSSOM
3 DROPS HONEYSUCKLE OIL

Honeysuckle Cream (p.76). Melt petroleum jelly in a bowl placed in a pan of hot water. Add blossom. Heat mixture in a pan of simmering water for 30 minutes. Strain, add essential oil and cool. Pack in a lidded jar.

POTPOURRIS FOR SACHETS

CALAMUS MIX

❋

1pt (500g) CALAMUS LEAVES
1pt (500g) ROSE-SCENTED GERANIUM (PELARGONIUM) LEAVES
1oz (30g) LAVENDER
1oz (30g) ORRIS ROOT POWDER
GRATED RIND OF AN ORANGE
1 TEASPOON CINNAMON POWDER
4 DROPS GERANIUM OIL
2 DROPS ORANGE OIL
2 DROPS ROSE OIL

The Fresh Blue Sachets (p.82) and the Lace Sachets (p.83) contain this spicy dry potpourri.

LAVENDER MIX

❋

2pt (1 liter) LAVENDER
1oz (30g) ORRIS ROOT POWDER
2 TEASPOONS CLOVES
6 DROPS LAVENDER OIL
2 DROPS CLOVE OIL

The Blue-flowered Ribbon Sachet (p.74) is filled with this pleasing dry potpourri, which complements that of the Lavender-blue Pomander (p.75).

ROSE MIX

❋

2pt (1 liter) ROSE PETALS
1oz (30g) ORRIS ROOT POWDER
6 DROPS ROSE OIL
2 DROPS CLARY SAGE OIL

The Pink-flowered Ribbon Sachet (p.74) is filled with a dry potpourri that is rose-scented with a hint of musk, a perfect match to the Rose-red Pomander (p.75).

CARMELITE MIX

❋

1pt (500ml) ORANGE FLOWERS
1pt (500ml) LEMON BALM
2oz (60g) CHOPPED ANGELICA ROOT
1oz (30g) ORRIS ROOT POWDER
PEEL OF 2 LEMONS
1 GRATED NUTMEG
2 TEASPOONS CLOVES
2 TEASPOONS CORIANDER SEEDS
1 TEASPOON CINNAMON POWDER
4 DROPS NEROLI OIL
2 DROPS CORIANDER OIL
2 DROPS LEMON OIL

The Nightdress Case (p.72), the Ribbon & Lace Sachet (p.75) and the Needlework Cushion (pp.82-83) are all scented with this soothing dry potpourri.

MOTH-REPELLENT MIX

❋

2oz (60g) ROSEMARY
2oz (60g) TANSY
2oz (60g) WORMWOOD
1oz (30g) ORRIS ROOT POWDER
1 CRUSHED CINNAMON STICK
2 TEASPOONS CLOVES
4 DROPS ROSEMARY OIL

The Drawer Liners (p.83) are scented with this dry potpourri, which is also suitable for filling small sachets.

CAMPHOR & LAVENDER MIX

❋

4oz (120g) LAVENDER
2oz (60g) MINT
1oz (30g) FINE-GROUND GUM BENZOIN
1 TEASPOON CLOVES
1 TEASPOON CORIANDER SEEDS
1 CRUMBLED STAR ANISE
3 DROPS CAMPHOR OIL
3 DROPS LAVENDER OIL

The Embroidered Squares and the Hearts & Lace Sachets (p.82) are filled with this dry potpourri, which has a wonderful piercing scent. The Blue & White Hearts (p.74) also contain this basic mix but larkspur flowers are used in place of the mint, which makes the fragrance slightly less sharp.

POTPOURRIS FOR PILLOWS & CUSHIONS

SLEEP MIX

1 1/2pt (750ml) Hops
1/2pt (250ml) Lemon Balm
2oz (60g) Lavender
1oz (30g) Orris Root Powder
1 Teaspoon Cloves
1 Teaspoon Crushed Cardamom Seeds
2 Drops Clove Oil
2 Drops Lavender Oil
2 Drops Melissa (Lemon Balm) Oil

*The **Scatter Cushions** and **Sleep Pillow** (pp.72-73) are filled with this dry potpourri.*

POTPOURRIS FOR CONTAINERS

FLORAL MIX

1pt (500ml) Mixed Garden Flowers
1pt (500ml) Bay Leaves & Myrtle
2oz (60g) Lavender
1oz (30g) Orris Root Powder
1 Broken Cinnamon Stick
2 Teaspoons Cloves
2 Drops Carnation Oil
2 Drops Lemon Oil
2 Drops Rose Oil

*The **Large Terracotta Jar** (p.80) contains this dry mix. The **Matching Terracotta Jars** (p.81) are also filled with the same basic mix but with roses and peppermint as the main ingredients.*

POTPOURRIS FOR DISPLAY

MUSKY MIX

2pt (1 liter) Mixed Pink Flowers
2oz (60g) Lavender
1oz (30g) Orris Root Powder
2 Teaspoons Cinnamon Powder
3 Crushed Tonka Beans
1 Chopped Vanilla Pod
Peel of an Orange
4 Drops Carnation Oil
2 Drops Orange Oil

*The **Shallow Dish** (p.78) displays this musky but sharp dry potpourri.*

✿ Flower Ribbon Sachets *These sachets are ideal in the wardrobe or on display.*

LUXURIOUS MIX

2pt (1 liter) Stock-pot Petals
1oz (30g) Lavender
1oz (30g) Orris Root Powder
2 Teaspoons Cinnamon Powder
1/2 Chopped Vanilla Pod
1/2 Teaspoon Crushed Cloves
4 Drops Rose Oil
2 Drops Lavender Oil
Rose Buds & Bluebells to Decorate

*The **Nautilus Shell** (p.79) is filled with this rose- and lavender-scented moist potpourri, which is ideal for the bedroom.*

FLOWER & HERB MIX

1pt (500ml) Roses & Rose Petals
1pt (500ml) Flame-of-the-Forest
2oz (60g) Mixed Sweet Herbs
1oz (30g) Orris Root Powder
1/2 Teaspoon Crushed Cardamom Seeds
4 Drops Any Floral Oil
2 Drops Peppermint Oil

*The **Small Silver Bowl** (p.79) displays this mainly floral dry potpourri.*

The Nursery

❦

THERE IS NO BETTER WAY to encourage a love of the natural world in your child than by taking him or her into the garden to gather herbs and flowers that will ultimately be used to fill toys. Your child will remember plant names and fragrances with enthusiasm, and will love to be involved in making the toys. There are many playthings you can make that can also be scented. Simply adapt any ideas you have to include either a potpourri stuffing or a scented sachet. For example, dolls full of lavender, herb-stuffed teddy bears and a curious Puff Ball caterpillar, which is made of patchwork circles each filled with a different mix. Nothing could be more exciting to a child than an array of fragrances. In the nineteenth century it was recommended that nurseries be scented with the spicy aromas of cloves, nutmeg, cinnamon and caraway.

However, children soon discover their own favorite scents. These often relate to the familiar smell of the kitchen – orange and lemon, and peppermint and spearmint are all popular. These fresh aromas are ideal for the nursery because they are also quite soothing; add one or two of them, together with a little lavender, to a hop-stuffed cushion and you will have a traditional "sleep pillow." Hot-water-bottle covers or nightdress cases are easily made and can be perfumed by tucking a sachet inside the case or into a pocket sewn on the front. Sachets can range from rose-scented dolls to tiny lavender teddy bears and from little herby chicks to simple spicy squares. Bright colors are beloved of children and look delightful in the nursery. Of course, there are some children who prefer subdued colors and more sophisticated perfumes. So work with them when scenting and decorating their rooms.

❦ FRAGRANT TOYS & PILLOWS
Brighten and perfume the nursery by making scented toys (above) or fill pillows with fragrant mixes (left).

❦

❀❀ NOT ALL THE TOYS SHOWN
HERE ARE SUITABLE FOR PLAYING
WITH, AND CARE SHOULD BE TAKEN
TO DISPLAY THEM OUT OF THE
REACH OF VERY YOUNG CHILDREN.

❀ GREEN TEDDY BEAR
*Made from nylon lace and
filled with a lemon-scented
mix, this teddy bear is
only suitable for
decorative purposes.*

❀ SLEEP TEDDY
BEAR *This teddy is
filled with a soothing
peppermint and hop
mixture. Hang him out of
reach over the bed or crib.*

❀ CHICKS & TEDDY
BEARS *Made to match
the bigger toys, these
herb-scented sachets
can be tucked
between clothes
or bedlinen.*

❀ MOTHER HEN *Filled
with an herby mix, this
colorful hen looks lovely
when displayed with
her two yellow chicks.*

❧ AROMATIC TOYS ❧

Aromatic soft toys add a new dimension to the nursery. Hang a lavender doll in the nursery and the scent of lavender will fill the room. Teddy bear and chicken sachets are simple to make and they, too, will gently perfume the air; alternatively, tucked into drawers they will sweeten the contents. If you are making toys for very young children, encase the potpourri in fire-resistant batting to make them safe to play with, or display them out of reach.

❁ FLORAL DOLLS *Easily made from tiny scraps of material and filled with rose petals, these sachet dolls are perfect for putting in chests of drawers and cupboards.*

❁ DAINTY DOLLS *Embroidered faces, lace and ribbons transform these simple sachets into lovely dolls.*

❁ LAVENDER LILY *This enchanting doll is made with net material and filled with lavender. She is the ideal decoration for a little girl's room and will imbue the room with the fragrance of lavender.*

❧ TRADITIONAL CRAFTS ❧

P ATCHWORK AND WICKERWORK are among the many crafts that can provide inspiration for scented decorations in the nursery. The long tradition of these crafts ensures that most of the items you choose will blend in with almost any nursery. Sew your patchwork using cloth of bright, primary colors and all children will be captivated. Plain wickerwork can be painted and varnished to make it more attractive. Children generally like lemon, rose, lavender and herbal scents – peppermint in particular is very popular – so it is best to make most of your mixtures in this scent range unless your child has a special preference.

❀ CATERPILLAR
Charming and bound to please any child, this caterpillar is made from traditional Puff Balls that are filled with a light, herbal mix.

❀ NURSERY
GARLAND *Tightly stuffed Puff Balls are glued on top of a wickerwork base to produce this lovely, brightly colored and strongly scented garland, which is ideal for displaying on a shelf or hanging on the nursery wall.*

❋ CANEWORK
CHICKEN *This
chicken is ideal for
a nursery as children
cannot spill the pot-
pourri but the lemon
scent will easily filter
through the cane.*

❋ PATCHWORK
SACHETS *Sachets,
lightly filled with
a rose and lavender
potpourri or a delicate
herbal mixture, are ideal
for tucking into drawers
and the pockets of clothes
to keep them sweetly scented.*

❀ HOT–WATER–BOTTLE
COVER *A simple and useful
bedtime accessory, this hot-
water-bottle cover is scented
with sachets placed in
the little front pocket.*

❀ TEDDY
BEARS *These
sachets are ideal
for providing a
gentle perfume.
Fill each teddy
with a different
mix to vary
the fragrance.*

❀ GINGHAM
PAJAMA CASE *A
lovely pajama case
brightens the crib
during the day
and scents the
nightwear kept
inside it.*

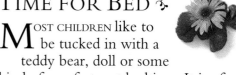

⊰ TIME FOR BED ⊱

MOST CHILDREN like to be tucked in with a teddy bear, doll or some kind of comforter at bedtime. It is often a very simple object that reassures children who are afraid of the dark if they wake in the night. Regular bedtime accessories, such as hot-water-bottle covers, pillows and pajama cases, are all ideal companions, and are easily scented with sachets or by putting potpourri inside an envelope of stuffing, which is then placed inside the cloth cover.

❀ COORDINATING ACCESSORIES *Made with matching material and filled with complementary pot-pourris, this pillow and pajama case are wonderful additions to the nursery.*

❀ STRAW TOYS
Little straw toys are scented by being placed in a potpourri or by rubbing them with a little essential oil.

CHAMOMILE & LEMON MIX

1pt (500ml) CHAMOMILE FLOWERS
1pt (500ml) LEMON VERBENA
2oz (60g) ROSEMARY
1oz (30g) ORRIS ROOT POWDER
2 TEASPOONS CLOVES
1 TEASPOON CINNAMON POWDER
4 DROPS LEMON OIL
2 DROPS CHAMOMILE OIL
2 DROPS ROSEMARY OIL

*The **Green Teddy** (p.88) is
filled with this dry potpourri.
It is lemon-scented with herby
chamomile overtones.*

NURSERY SLEEP MIX

1pt (500ml) MIXED
MEADOWSWEET, MINTS
& ROSEMARY
1pt (500ml) HOPS
2oz (60g) LAVENDER
1oz (30g) ORRIS
ROOT POWDER
2 DROPS LAVENDER OIL
2 DROPS ROSEMARY OIL
2 DROPS PEPPERMINT OIL

*The **Sleep Teddy** (p.88) is filled
with this delicious and soothing
dry potpourri, which will
fill the nursery with a
relaxing fragrance.*

POTPOURRIS FOR
CUSHIONS & CASES

ROSE & PINE MIX

1pt (500ml) ROSE PETALS
1pt (500ml) MIXED CONIFER TIPS
& PINE NEEDLES
2oz (60g) LAVENDER
1oz (30g) ORRIS
ROOT POWDER
2 TEASPOONS
ALLSPICE BERRIES
3 DROPS ROSE OIL
2 DROPS LAVENDER OIL
2 DROPS PINE OIL

*The **Gingham Pajama Case**
(p.92) is scented with this dry potpourri.
The rose petals make the mix sweet
while the pine needles give it
crisp overtones, producing
a delicious scent.*

HOPS & MINT SLEEP MIX

1pt (500ml) HOPS
1pt (500ml) MIXED ALECOST & MINT
2oz (60g) LAVENDER
1oz (30g) ORRIS ROOT POWDER
GRATED RIND OF A LEMON
1 TEASPOON CRUSHED
CARDAMOM SEEDS
2 DROPS LEMON OIL
2 DROPS PEPPERMINT OIL
2 DROPS LAVENDER OIL

*The **Coordinating Accessories** (p.93)
are scented with this dry potpourri.
It is a soothing sleep mix, wonderful for
scenting pajamas and nighties.*

POTPOURRIS FOR
SACHETS

ROSEMARY, THYME
& CARAWAY MIX

1pt (500ml) ROSEMARY
1pt (500ml) THYME
1oz (30g) ORRIS ROOT POWDER
2 TEASPOONS CARAWAY SEEDS
3 DROPS ROSEMARY OIL
3 DROPS THYME OIL

❀ TEDDY BEAR
SACHET *Teddy bear
sachets can be filled
with any mix and
are always charming.*

❧ RECIPES ☙

POTPOURRIS FOR TOYS
& DECORATIONS

FRESH MIX

2pt (1 liter) MIXED SWEET HERBS
2oz (60g) LAVENDER
1oz (30g) ORRIS ROOT POWDER
2 TEASPOONS CARAWAY SEEDS
2 TEASPOONS CRUSHED
CARDAMOM SEEDS
4 DROPS CLARY SAGE OIL
2 DROPS LAVENDER OIL

*The **Mother Hen** (p.88) is stuffed
with this herbal dry potpourri, which
will freshen the air in the nursery.*

RED & YELLOW MIX

1pt (500ml) YELLOW
EVERLASTING FLOWERS
1pt (500ml) RED COCKSCOMB FLOWERS
2oz (60g) ROSEMARY
1oz (30g) FINE-GROUND GUM BENZOIN
2 TEASPOONS CRUSHED ALLSPICE BERRIES
1 BROKEN CINNAMON STICK
6 DROPS LEMON OIL
2 DROPS ROSEMARY OIL

*The **Canework Chicken** (p.91) is
filled with this dry potpourri. This
brightly colored dry potpourri
can be displayed out of reach in
the nursery or placed in a
child-proof container.*

BASIC SPICE MIX

1oz (30g) Crushed Cloves
1oz (30g) Caraway Seeds
1oz (30g) Crushed Cardamom Seeds
1oz (30g) Crushed Allspice Berries
1oz (30g) Orris Root Powder
4 Drops Clove Oil
2 Drops Lavender Oil

ROSEMARY MIX

2pt (1 liter) Rosemary
1oz (30g) Orris Root Powder
4 Drops Rosemary Oil

❀ Nursery
Garland
*This Puff Ball
garland is lovely
in the nursery and
is popular with
young children.*

MARJORAM & LEMON THYME MIX

2pt (1 liter) Mixed Lemon Thyme
& Marjoram
1oz (30g) Orris Root Powder
4 Drops Lemon Oil
2 Drops Marjoram Oil

LEMON VERBENA MIX

2pt (1 liter) Lemon Verbena
1oz (30g) Orris Root Powder
6 Drops Lemon Oil

SIMPLE LAVENDER MIX

2pt (1 liter) Lavender
1oz (30g) Orris Root Powder
6 Drops Lavender Oil

*The assorted sachets on pp.88-93 are
filled with these potpourris. They
are unsophisticated but lovely
and are all ideal for filling small
sachets that are to be placed
in hot-water-bottle covers and
in drawers and cupboards.
Each recipe makes enough
potpourri for 8 sachets.*

PUFF BALLS

*Puff Balls are a traditional
patchwork design. Cut out a circle
of cloth and make a small hem all
around the edge using fairly large
stitches. Fill the center of the circle with
the mix you desire, then gather the
thread, tie the ends and tuck them into
the center of the puff. Continue making
puffs in this way until you have
enough for your design. The puff
can either be stuffed tightly or loosely
depending on the desired
effect. Puff Balls are
very easy to make
and children will
love to help.*

PUFF BALL CATERPILLAR

Caterpillar *(p.90). Lightly fill Puff
Balls with dried herbs, flatten them and
sew them together through their centers.*

GERANIUM & LAVENDER MIX

1pt (500ml) Ground Ivy Leaves
1pt (500ml) Scented Geranium
(Pelargonium) Leaves
2oz (60g) Lavender
1oz (30g) Orris Root Powder
2 Teaspoons Cinnamon
Powder
2 Teaspoons Ground Cloves
4 Drops Geranium Oil
2 Drops Lavender Oil
2 Drops Ylang-ylang oil

The Nursery Garland *(p.90) is filled
with this dry potpourri. This strongly
scented mix is popular among children.*

THE BATHROOM

BEAUTIFUL, perfumed potpourris, pretty bouquets and garlands, baskets of flowers and stunning botanical friezes will transform any bathroom. Shells, sea glass, mosses, lichens, flowers, and silks and satins can all be found in wonderful shades of aquamarine, which, when they are mixed with mauve-blues, produce diffused, underwater colors that are ideal for the bathroom. Create contrasts by adding touches of pink and dark red, or yellow and orange to these hues. Large Abalone shells, with their wonderful, iridescent green linings, make beautiful containers for potpourris. Decorated with whole flowers and spices they become pretty, textured tapestries. Try filling a large terracotta basket with dried flowers. Add artificially dyed flowers in shades of turquoise, jade and pink to accentuate the colors

❀ BATH LUXURIES *Treat yourself to a fragrant bath (left) by adding rose petals and home-made bath oil to the water and using essential oil soap.*

of the sea. Make substantial and opulent bouquets or tiny nosegays. Embellish garlands with small, scented shells and sea glass, fragrant flowers and even seaweed. Alternatively, adorn your wall with a luxuriant frieze – create a delicate landscape of pressed flowers, mosses and lichens. Use a floral sealer to protect dried-flower arrangements from the steamy atmosphere. Mix floral scents with sharp lemon, pine, geranium and orange to refresh their sweetness. Anise and orange makes an interesting combination, as does rose and orange. On the other hand, you may prefer the sweet oriental perfumes of ylang-ylang or exquisite jasmine. Store home-made bath essences, oils, shampoos and toilet vinegars in antique bottles and decorate them with dried flowers and ribbons to add to the overall charm of the bathroom.

❧ SACHETS & FRIEZE ❧

THERE ARE MANY different and effective ways of decorating the bathroom with scented displays. Hang sachets from the wall, over faucets and from door and window handles. Fill the sachets with your favorite scents, complementing those of your soaps and shampoos. Pressed-flower collages are also effective. A frieze, such as the one below, adds individuality and color to the bathroom and will lend the room a gentle perfume.

✿ SEA SACHETS
Filled with a floral mix, these sachets are made with strips of silk.

✿ SWINGING SCENT *Small, lemon-scented sachets, tied to a wooden ring, are ideal for hanging from the curtain rod.*

❁ BLUE BELLES
A jasmine pot-pourri fills these pretty hanging sachets.

❁ RUBY SACHET
A pressed-flower decoration adds the finishing touch to this charming sachet.

❁ FLORAL SQUARES *Perfect for display or for scenting towels in the linen cupboard, these sachets are filled with rosemary and southernwood.*

❁ FRIEZE *This frieze is made by arranging delicate pressed flowers in a landscape of mosses. The mosses are scented with chamomile oil to provide a long-lasting fragrance.*

❧ POSIES & WREATHS ❧

THE SEASIDE is a particularly apt and traditional theme to follow when decorating the bathroom. In your posies and wreaths use colors that are in keeping with the seaside – turquoise, blue and sea-green are ideal as they evoke clear skies and enticing water. Flowers that have been dyed blue or green will not look out of place, especially if used sparingly to highlight the appearance of the mix. Add shells and pebbles to the plant material, to complete the theme. All sorts of scents suit the bathroom and, although the fragrance you choose should not be overpowering, it can be quite strong. Hang posies and wreaths on walls, from the ceiling, on the side of the bath, or on the mirror.

ANAPHALIS (DYED JADE)

LAVENDER

❀ LARGE POSY *Among the medley of flowers used in this pretty bouquet are everlasting flowers and Queen-Anne's-lace. Rose oil, dropped in the centers of the rose buds, mingles with the perfume of the lavender.*

❀ PETITE POSY *This charming little posy, which matches the seaside wreath in color, is scented with star anise and orange oil.*

❀ SEA GLASS *These pretty glass fragments were scented by steeping them in a jar of perfumed essence.*

ANAPHALIS
(DYED PINK)

ROSE

❀ SEASIDE WREATH *This wreath is scented with lemon and bergamot oils and is reminiscent of the seaside in its display of shells and colors such as sea-green, cream and turquoise.*

❀ FORMAL CIRCLET *The scent of roses and geranium oil pervades this circlet of red roses and pink- and jade-dyed anaphalis.*

QUEEN-ANNE'S-
LACE

STATICE

❀ BUBBLE BATHS
*Floral or spicy
perfumes can be
used to make
luxurious
bubble baths.*

❧ SOAPS & SHAMPOOS ❧

SPECIAL SOAPS and shampoos, bath oils, bubble baths and toilet vinegars are lovely to have in the bathroom. All these toiletries are simple to make at home and can be scented with your favorite fragrances. Decorate the bottles with dried flowers and pretty ribbons, and they will look lovely arranged on the shelves and around the bath.

❈ TOILET VINEGAR
*Geranium leaves and
oakmoss scent this
toilet vinegar (far right).*

❈ HAIR RINSE *After
shampooing, a chamomile
hair rinse (center) is perfect
for reviving the hair.*

❈ BATH OIL
*(right) This
relaxing bath
oil is scented
with orange
and rose
essential oils.*

❈ DRY SHAMPOO *Scented
with rosemary, this dry
shampoo (left) quickly
refreshes your hair.*

❈ BATH BAGS *Filled with
dried herbs, these sachets
(above) will make your bath
water scented and refreshing.*

❈ ESSENTIAL OIL SOAP
*These soaps are lovely
for guests or for your
own personal use.*

❀ TERRACOTTA BASKET *This terracotta basket is filled with an assortment of dried plant material, including larkspur, dyed anaphalis and woodrush. The arrangement is scented with a sweet, tangy blend of Bois de Rose oil and orange oil.*

❀ GLASS JAR *Layers of larkspur, lavender, flame-of-the-forest and rose petals, decorated with blue- and pink-dyed anaphalis, fill this jar. Each layer is scented with 4 drops of rose oil and 4 drops of clary sage oil for a rich, musky fragrance.*

❧ DESIGNS WITH DRIED FLOWERS ❧

LARGE ARRANGEMENTS OF LONG-LASTING DRIED FLOWERS will transform a bathroom. Use your creative abilities to produce stunning displays – perhaps a basket brimming with pretty, chintzy flowers, or a formal porcelain container full of boldly colored botanicals. Try using artificially dyed flowers: they are ideal for the bathroom as their bright colors will not fade in the steamy atmosphere. If you prefer more subtle colors make sure that they will not be lost among all the other colors in the bathroom. Perfume your design by spreading a layer of potpourri over the top of the dry foam in which your flowers are arranged, or put a drop or two of a potpourri reviver or an essential oil on to the back of some of the larger flowers.

❀ INVIGORATING MIX
*The sharp pine and
lemon fragrance of this
elegant potpourri (left)
is softened by a gentle
floral background of
rose and lavender.*

❧ POTPOURRIS ❧

POTPOURRIS MADE FOR THE BATHROOM look lovely
when displayed on the windowsill or bathroom
dresser. Try to re-create the perfume of your home-
made bath sachets or soaps so that the scents enhance
one another – there is nothing better than being
surrounded by your favorite scent when you are soaking
in a bath at the end of a busy day. If you prefer to take a
quick, invigorating shower rather than a bath,
try fresh citrus or spicy perfumes to wake
you up along with your wash. Heady,
exotic fragrances are wonderful in a large
and luxurious bathroom. A small, utilitarian
bathroom is best scented with lighter, floral
fragrances. Re-create the seasons by using perfumes
that evoke them – the warm days of summer will come flooding
back as you inhale the fragrance of roses and lavender. Present
your potpourri in a container that is in keeping with the room.
Shells, old-fashioned chamber pots and pottery soap dishes
are ideal choices. Make sure that your container complements
the colors of your potpourri and the decor of your bathroom.

PERFUMED
SOAP

❁ INGREDIENTS: LAVENDER,
MOCK ORANGE BLOSSOM, ROSES,
ROSE PETALS AND STAR ANISE.

❁ INGREDIENTS: ANAPHALIS,
BLUEBELLS, LARKSPUR, ROSE BUDS
AND ROSE PETALS.

❁ INGREDIENTS: ANAPHALIS (DYED
PINK AND JADE), 'DE CAEN'
ANEMONES, HYDRANGEA (DYED
DARK GREEN) AND MALLOW.

❁ SPICY ROSE MIX
Sweet-smelling
rose buds and
spicy cinnamon
sticks perfume
this formal
but delicate
potpourri (left)

❁ ORIENTAL MIX *Patchouli*
is used to enrich and enhance
the sweet and heady oriental
perfume of this potpourri
(left). It is a long-lasting
mix as most of the ingredients
are artificially colored and
therefore remain bright
over a long period.

❧ RECIPES ❧

FOR THE BATH

ROSE & ORANGE BATH OIL

2$\frac{1}{2}$fl oz (75ml) SUNFLOWER OIL
1 TABLESPOON HERBAL SHAMPOO
1 TABLESPOON ROSE OIL
1 TEASPOON ORANGE OIL

Bath Oils *(p.103). Put sunflower oil, herbal shampoo and essential oils in a bottle with a stopper and shake well. Leave for 2 weeks shaking daily. Use 1 tablespoon in the bath, pouring it under running hot water tap.*
VARIATION: *To make pine bath oil use 1 tablespoon of pine oil and 1 teaspoon of lemon oil instead of the rose and orange oils.*

GERANIUM & OAKMOSS TOILET VINEGAR

1pt (500ml) CIDER VINEGAR
(PREFERABLY A PALE ONE)
1pt (500ml) SPRING OR PURIFIED WATER
3oz (90g) FRESH GERANIUM
(PELARGONIUM) LEAVES
1oz (30g) OAKMOSS
4 DROPS GERANIUM OIL

Toilet Vinegar *(p.103). Put geranium leaves and oakmoss in a container. Mix vinegar and water and heat to just below boiling point then pour over geranium leaves and oakmoss. Seal container with plastic wrap and leave to infuse for 24 hours. Strain, add essential oils, bottle and cork. Shake well. Use about 1 cupful in the bath or dab on the body. Shake bottle before use.*

FLORAL BUBBLE BATH

$\frac{1}{2}$pt (250ml) ORGANIC WASHING LIQUID
$\frac{1}{2}$pt (250ml) PURIFIED WATER
2 TEASPOONS ANY FLORAL ESSENTIAL OIL
2 DROPS FOOD COLORING (OPTIONAL)

Bubble Baths *(p.102). Mix organic washing liquid with purified water. Add essential oils and food coloring and mix well. Bottle. Use 1 tablespoon per bath.*
VARIATION: *Substitute 2 teaspoons of clove oil for the floral oil for a spicy bubble bath.*

❀ LARGE POSY
This lavender- and rose-scented posy is lovely in the bathroom.

BATH BAGS

2oz (60g) DRIED FLOWERS
1oz (30g) LAVENDER (OPTIONAL)
$\frac{1}{2}$oz (15g) ROLLED OATS
GRATED RIND OF $\frac{1}{2}$ A LEMON

Bath Bags *(pp.102-3). Put the mixed ingredients in small, cotton bags. Lavender enhances the perfume; oats make the water creamy.*

FOR THE BODY

DRY SHAMPOO

4oz (120g) ORRIS ROOT POWDER
1oz (30g) UNPERFUMED TALC
4 DROPS ROSEMARY OIL

Dry Shampoo *(p.103). Mix ingredients together thoroughly. Rub into hair, leave for 5 minutes and brush out.*

ESSENTIAL OIL SOAP

¹/₂pt (250ml) Boiling Water
10oz (300g) Unscented Soap
6 Drops any Essential Oil
4 Drops Food Coloring

Essential Oil Soap (p.103).
Grate soap into a bowl, add other
ingredients and knead well. Leave to
harden. Place soap between plastic
wrap, roll out to ³/₄in (2cm)
thick and cut tablets of soap with
a pastry cutter. Wrap in plastic
wrap and leave for 24 hours.
Remove plastic wrap and allow
soap to dry until hard.
Finally, polish with cotton
wool soaked in essential oil.

POTPOURRIS FOR DISPLAY

SPICY ROSE MIX

1pt (500ml) Rose Buds
1pt (500ml) Rose Petals
2oz (60g) Lavender
1oz (30g) Orris Root Powder
2 Cinnamon Sticks
1 Teaspoon Cloves
3 Drops Geranium Oil
3 Drops Rose Oil
White Anaphalis & Blue
Larkspur to Decorate

*The Spicy Rose Mix (pp.106-7)
is a dry potpourri with a fragrance of
soft roses, spicy cinnamon and cloves.*

INVIGORATING MIX

1pt (500ml) Whole Roses
1pt (500ml) Mixed Lemon Balm, Lemon
Verbena & Chopped Pine Needles
1oz (30g) Lavender
1oz (30g) Fine-ground Gum Benzoin
Peel of a Lemon
2 Teaspoons Crushed Allspice Berries
6 Star Anise
4 Drops Pine Oil
2 Drops Lemon Oil
2 Drops Rose Oil
Mock Orange Blossom
to Decorate

*The Invigorating Mix (p.106) is a
dry potpourri in which several exciting
fragrances are blended together.*

ORIENTAL MIX

2pt (1 liter) Mixed Pink- & Jade-dyed
Anaphalis, Dark Green-sprayed
Hydrangea Flowers & Black
Mallow Flowers
1oz (30g) Scented Geranium
(Pelargonium) Leaves
1oz (30g) Orris Root Powder
2 Teaspoons Cinnamon Powder
¹/₂ Teaspoon Cloves
4 Drops Narcissus Oil
(or any heady floral oil)
2 Drops Ylang-ylang Oil
1 Drop Patchouli Oil
'de Caen' Anemones & Purple
Statice to Decorate

*The Oriental Mix (p.107) is a sweet
colorful dry potpourri.*

POTPOURRIS FOR SACHETS

CITRUS & FLORAL MIX

¹/₂pt (250ml) Rose Petals
¹/₂pt (250ml) Lavender
1oz (30g) Hyssop
Grated Rind of ¹/₂ an Orange
Grated Rind of ¹/₂ a Lemon
1 Teaspoon Grated Nutmeg
4 Drops Vetiver Oil
2 Drops Lavender Oil
2 Drops Rose Oil

*The Sea Sachets (p.98) are stuffed with this
lovely floral dry potpourri, which
has tangy orange and lemon overtones.*

INSECT-DETERRENT MIX

1pt (500ml) Rosemary
1pt (500ml) Southernwood
1oz (30g) Lavender
1oz (30g) Fine-ground Gum Benzoin
2oz (60g) Cloves
2 Teaspoons Cinnamon Powder
4 Drops Rosemary Oil
2 Drops Lavender Oil

*The Floral Squares (p.99) are filled with
this dry potpourri.*

ORIENTAL JASMINE MIX

1pt (500ml) Jasmine Flowers
& Rose Petals
1pt (500ml) Lavender
1oz (30g) Fine-ground Gum Benzoin
1oz (30g) Crumbled Cinnamon
1oz (30g) Vetiver
Grated Rind of an Orange
1 Crumbled Star Anise
¹/₄ Chopped Vanilla Pod
4 Drops Jasmine Oil
4 Drops Lavender Oil
2 Drops Ylang-ylang Oil

*The Blue Belles and the Ruby
Sachet (p.98) contain this mix.*

HEADY LEMON MIX

1pt (500ml) Carnations
1pt (500ml) Lemon Verbena
2oz (60g) Basil
1oz (30g) Orris Root Powder
2 Tonka Beans
¹/₂ Chopped Vanilla Pod
4 Drops Carnation Oil
2 Drops Lemon Oil
2 Drops Patchouli Oil

*The Swinging Scent Sachets
(p.98) are filled with this
dry potpourri.*

Bath
Oil

BASIC TECHNIQUES

THE TECHNIQUES USED to make all the fragrant delights in this book are quite simple to follow and, once you have mastered them you can become more ambitious in the things you create. It is best to begin by learning how to make both dry and moist potpourris, for, in doing so, you will understand the fundamental rules of creating and holding a fragrance. Potpourri consists of five main groups of elements. First come the dried botanicals that form the bulk of the mix. In a dry potpourri these might be rose petals or other scented petals or flowers, leaves, roots, seeds or woods; this group can consist of dried botanicals that are attractive but not scented. In a moist potpourri rose petals are cured with salt (and possibly brown sugar and brandy too). The resulting "stock pot" makes up the first group of botanicals.

Second come the complementary sweet herbs. Usually just lavender is used although rosemary and other herbs can be included. Third come the fixatives. I have used mainly orris root powder or fine-ground gum benzoin. Fixatives are essential for holding the fragrance and without them the potpourri quickly loses its scent. Fourth come the spices that add a subtle and interesting depth to the bouquet of the mix. Finally come the essential oils, the perfume of which dominates the potpourri. Essential oils are concentrated perfumes extracted from aromatic plant materials. You will also need some lovely whole flowers and leaves, and possibly some whole spices, in order to decorate the whole mix. Scented colognes, essences, waters and oils are made by immersing fragrant plant materials in alcohol, vinegar or oil, that extracts the perfume from them.

❈ EXTRACTING PERFUMES *Drying leaves and flowers (left) or making scented oils (above) are just two ways of using the fragrant elements in plants.*

✦ FRESH FLOWERS ❧

BRIGHTEN AND PERFUME any room in the house by decorating it with fresh, scented flowers and aromatic greenery.

Gather the fragrant plant materials when the sun has dried the dew on them but has not yet made the delicate flowers wilt: this is usually around midday. Choose flowers and leaves that are in good condition; if they are damaged they will quickly deteriorate and you will have to renew the display.

Start by making a simple, fan-shaped arrangement, such as the one shown here, and then experiment with other shapes as your confidence grows.

MAKING A FAN-SHAPED ARRANGEMENT

1 *Gather the tools and ingredients you need: a knife to cut the wet foam, scissors or pruning shears to trim stems and leaves, a container and the plant materials.*

2 *Shape the foam to fit the container. Place it inside and moisten it well. Starting from the center back, make a basic fan shape. Then fill out toward the front.*

❀ WINTER GREENERY
This display of scented evergreens, with fragrant jonquils and daphne to provide color, is arranged in a classic fan shape.

❧ DRIED FLOWERS ❧

FLOWERS CAN BE DRIED and used in dried-flower designs and potpourris. A simple way to dry them is to remove most of the
leaves, make a bunch – varying the height of the flowerheads – and
hang it upside-down in a warm, dry, shady place. Drying with silica
gel is more complicated but the flowers keep their colors better.

❀ HANG-DRYING *Bunches of
flowers hung in a warm, shady
place make a lovely display.*

DRYING WITH SILICA GEL

1 *Fill the bottom of an airtight container
with 1in (2cm) of silica gel. With scissors or
pruning shears, remove the flowerheads.
Whole sprays of flowers may also be dried.*

2 *If you plan to add wire stems, insert a
pin in the back of each flower. Place them
face-up in the container. (Flat flowers,
such as daisies, may be placed face-down.)*

3 *Sprinkle silica gel between the petals and
over the flowers until they are covered with
1in (2cm) of gel. Remove the flowers in 3
to 4 days or when they are crispy dry.*

PRESSED FLOWERS

PRESSED PLANT MATERIALS can be used in many ways – to make collages and posters, to decorate old bottles and jars, and to embellish cards, notepaper, gift tags and bookmarks.

Almost any plant material – including mosses, seedheads and berries – can be pressed. The material you use must be in good condition and should not be picked when wet.

Gather the plant material as it becomes available. Arrange materials of similar thickness in each layer to ensure an even pressure is applied, but include a variety of plants so that you have plenty of choice when making your design.

For the best results dry the plant material quickly. Do this by placing three sheets of folded, recycled paper between the paper that contains the pressed plant materials and replace this paper regularly. The paper can be dried and reused.

When it is dry and crisp – after about two weeks – remove the material from the press and store it between sheets of recycled paper in a dry place so that it does not go moldy.

1 *Place a paper towel on the base of a piece of folded, recycled paper. Using tweezers, place the plant material on top, ensuring it does not overlap.*

2 *Cover with a paper towel, fold over the recycled paper and place in the press. When it is full, screw the press down.*

✤ FLOWER PRESS *This large press is ideal for those wishing to press a large amount of material. Smaller presses are available for the beginner.*

✤ PRESSED-FLOWER LAYER *These beautiful pressed flowers and leaves are ready to be used in a design.*

❧ POTPOURRI ❧

There are two basic ways of making potpourri: the dry method and the moist method. Dry potpourris are quick and easy to make and very attractive. Moist potpourris are more highly scented than dry potpourris and, although less attractive, can be stored in pretty containers that are perforated to allow the fragrance to escape. They are prepared in two stages: the making of the stock-pot, which provides the intense scent, and the mixing of the stock-pot with the dry ingredients.

MAKING A MOIST POTPOURRI

1 *Separate the rose petals and leave to dry for 2 days. Fill an airtight jar with petals in ²/₃ in (1¹/₂ cm) layers, sprinkling each layer with salt (if desired, also sprinkle with brown sugar and drops of brandy). Continue adding more petals as they become available over a season, pressing each layer down well.*

2 *Leave to cure for 2 months, draining off excess liquid, if necessary. Crumble the matured "stock-pot" into a bowl that contains the other ingredients. Store the resulting moist potpourri in an airtight jar for 3 weeks. Remove and display in an attractive perforated container.*

❀ **DRY POTPOURRI** *Decorate the finished dry potpourri with dried, whole flowers.*

❀ **FOR A MOIST POTPOURRI YOU WILL NEED:** A SUPPLY OF ROSE PETALS, BROWN SUGAR, BRANDY, COARSE SALT.

❀ **FOR A DRY POTPOURRI YOU WILL NEED:** 2pt (1liter) DRIED FLOWERS, LEAVES, ROOTS OR SEEDS, 1oz (30g) LAVENDER, 1oz (30g) ORRIS ROOT POWDER, 1 TEASPOON CINNAMON POWDER, 6 DROPS OF ESSENTIAL OIL.

MAKING A DRY POTPOURRI

1 *Place fixatives, such as orris root powder or ground gum benzoin, and any powdered spices in a bowl, add essential oils and rub the mix between fingers until well blended.*

2 *Blend the remaining dry ingredients together in a large bowl. Then add the combined fixatives and essential oils and stir the mixture well, using a wooden spoon.*

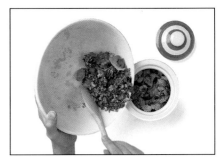

3 *Store the mixture in an airtight container or sealed plastic bag for 4-6 weeks. Remove, place in an attractive container and decorate with whole dried flowers.*

SCENTED PAPER

SCENTED STATIONERY is simple to make and adds a special touch to your correspondence. Make stationery using art paper, tearing it by hand to give it an attractive edge, or decorate shop-bought paper. Scent the paper by storing it with a sachet of potpourri for four weeks. Perfume and protect pressed-flower designs on bookmarks, gift tags and cards by painting them with melted, scented wax.

TEARING & SCENTING PAPER

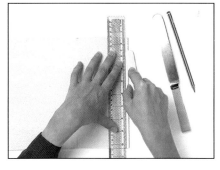

1 *Use a ruler to draw a line where you wish to tear the paper. Score line with a knife, fold and press along the fold. Turn paper over and repeat. Tear paper along the fold.*

2 *Staple together 2 tissues or paper towels on 3 sides to make a sachet. Fill it with potpourri and staple the last edge. Place the sachet and paper in a plastic bag and seal.*

❀ PAPER ARRAY *A wide variety of stationery can be made at home.*

❀ BLUE PAPER *Stored in a plastic bag with a potpourri sachet, this paper is imbued with scent.*

❧ DECORATED CANDLES ❧

PLAIN, WHITE DOMESTIC CANDLES are very attractive when they are decorated with pressed herbs and flowers. They are also the easiest candles to work with and are therefore suitable for the beginner to decorate. Select tall, spiky fronds or long flowerheads to decorate candles and avoid using bulky plant material, such as berries, as it is a potential fire hazard.

Take great care when you work with wax. Remember that melted wax is very flammable, so always use a low heat, and a deep, preferably double saucepan and do not allow the wax to touch the skin as it will cause painful burning.

After some practice, try decorating colored, tapering candles and eventually, try making your own candles. Beeswax candles can be bought in any craft shop.

❀ **FOR DECORATING DOMESTIC CANDLES YOU WILL NEED:** ENOUGH WAX TO COVER THE CANDLE WHEN IT IS DIPPED INTO THE SAUCEPAN, 6 DROPS OF WAX PERFUME OR ESSENTIAL OIL FOR EVERY 12OZ (360G) OF WAX, A SELECTION OF PRESSED FLOWERS & HERBS.

❀ SCENTED CANDLES *Although difficult for the beginner, with practice most of these candles can be made at home.*

1 *In a deep or double saucepan, gently melt wax over a low heat. Hold the candle by the wick and dip it into the wax. Allow to cool for 10 minutes and dip again.*

2 *When the candle is cool place the pressed herbs or flowers in position on it. Brush melted wax over the decoration to hold it in place and leave to cool for 10 minutes.*

3 *Dip the whole candle in the melted wax again to seal the decoration on the candle. Allow to cool completely and then polish the surface with a soft cloth or tissue.*

❁ CITRUS POMANDER
*The tangy scent of a
citrus pomander
is especially lovely
in the kitchen.*

**❁ FOR A FLORAL POMANDER YOU
WILL NEED:** A SPHERE OF DRY FOAM,
2oz (60g) OF LAVENDER FLOWERS,
A SELECTION OF SCENTED,
DRIED FLOWERS, GLUE, RIBBON.

**❁ FOR A CITRUS POMANDER YOU
WILL NEED:** A CITRUS FRUIT,
CLOVES, 1oz (30g) ORRIS ROOT
POWDER, 1oz (30g) CINNAMON
POWDER, 4 DROPS OF A TANGY
ESSENTIAL OIL, TAPE, RIBBON,
PINS, BEADS, A KNITTING NEEDLE.

❁ FLORAL
POMANDER
*Brighten and
scent any
room with a
floral pomander.*

⚜ POMANDERS ⚜

THERE ARE TWO basic types
of pomander: the citrus
pomander – a citrus fruit
decorated with cloves – and
the floral pomander – a sphere
of dry foam decorated with
dried flowers. Although time-
consuming, neither type is
difficult to learn how to make
and the end result is a lovely,
scented decoration.

MAKING A FLORAL POMANDER

1 *Using a paintbrush, dab patches of glue
on to the dry foam then carefully roll it
in the lavender flowers.*

2 *Using tweezers, pick up a dried flower,
dip the back into glue, then place on the
foam. Add flowers in small groups of a kind.*

MAKING A CITRUS POMANDER

1 *Divide the fruit into quarters with tape.
Starting next to the tape, working into the
center of each quarter, make holes ⅓in
(³/₄cm) apart. Place a clove in each hole.*

2 *Remove tape and put the pomander in a
bag containing a mixture of cinnamon, orris
root and essential oil. Shake well, remove,
brush off excess and wrap in tissue paper.*

3 *Leave in a dry place for 2 to 3 weeks.
Remove from tissue. Decorate with ribbon
and beads. (Omit step 2 should you wish
to have a purely citrus-scented pomander.)*

❧ DECORATIONS ❧

ONE OF THE MOST BEAUTIFUL and effective ways of using dried flowers is in a three-dimensional design. Such a decoration looks wonderful displayed in the center of a table but, of course, you can place them on many other flat surfaces to great effect.

The basic steps to follow are straightforward but the finished arrangement can be as intricate as you wish. Begin with a simple design and then experiment with more ambitious ideas.

MAKING A CENTERPIECE

3 *When the moss is in place, turn over the card and glue a border of lacy flowers on the underside. They should extend over the edge so that they are visible from the right side.*

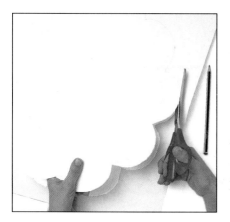

1 *With a pencil, mark your design on watercolor paper or white card. Use a template if you wish. Then cut carefully around the shape, using sharp scissors.*

4 *Trim any stalks off the flowers. Starting from the outside, gradually work inward, gluing the flowers to the moss in informal rows that follow the shape of the card.*

2 *Cover the whole of the shape with moss. Pick up the pieces of moss with tweezers, dip the backs into a saucer of glue and then stick them in place on the card.*

5 *Add scent by carefully dripping essential oil followed by oil of cloves into the center of a few of the flowers. Oil of cloves is a fixative, so the perfume will be long-lasting.*

❧ TOILETRIES ❧

COSMETIC CREAMS, perfumes, soaps, shampoos, bath oils and toilet waters are very simple to make in your own home. Most of the ingredients involved are natural and you can scent the products with your favorite fragrances. Food coloring can be added to alcohol- or vinegar-based toiletries to make them more visually attractive.

❀ **FOR JONQUIL COLOGNE YOU WILL NEED:** 1pt (500ml) VODKA, A SUPPLY OF FRESH, HIGHLY PERFUMED JONQUILS, 2 DROPS OF FOOD COLORING.

❀ **FOR BODY OIL YOU WILL NEED:** 1½ fl oz (50ml) ALMOND OIL, 10 DROPS OF ANY FLORAL ESSENTIAL OIL.

❀ SCENTED DELIGHTS
*All these cosmetics
and toiletries can be
made at home.*

MAKING JONQUIL COLOGNE

MAKING BODY OIL

1 *Pour in enough vodka to reach the shoulders of a bottle. Push the flowers into the bottle until the liquid is full. Cork and leave for 10 days, gently shaking daily.*

2 *Strain the liquid and replace the flowers with new ones. Repeat the whole process 3 times then bottle, add coloring and cork. Use glue to attach dried-flower decorations.*

This is one of the easiest toiletries to make. Pour almond oil into a bottle, add essential oil, place the stopper in the bottle and shake well. The oil is now ready to use.

❧ CUSHIONS & SACHETS ❧

LARGE, SCENTED CUSHIONS are easy to make and, once you have mastered the basic sewing techniques, smaller, more intricate, fragrant sachets will be well within your abilities.

Cushion covers are best made from materials that can be removed and washed, especially if the cushions will be in frequent use. Sachets are usually used purely as decoration so they can be made of more delicate materials, such as ribbon and lace.

❀ **FOR SACHETS & CUSHIONS YOU WILL NEED:** SCISSORS, PINS, NEEDLE, THREAD, CLOTH, LACE, RIBBON, BATTING, POTPOURRI.

MAKING A CUSHION

1 *Use a template to cut out 6 pieces of flame-proof batting. The shape should be ¹/₂in (1cm) smaller all-round than the cover you intend to use.*

2 *Holding or pinning the 6 pieces of batting together, sew around 3 sides of the shape, to make an envelope. (If the shape is round, leave a portion of the edge unsewn.)*

3 *Fill the batting envelope with a highly scented potpourri. Sew the final edge. Cut out and sew around 3 sides of the material you wish to use as a cover.*

❀ CUSHIONS
*Large, scented
cushions require
more sewing than
sachets but are less
fussy to make.*

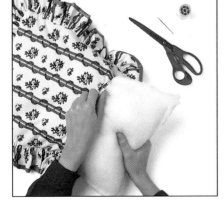

4 *Ease the envelope of batting into the
cushion cover and sew up the final edge.
(Use snaps or a zipper if you wish to be
able to remove the filling at a later date.)*

❀ BUTTERFLIES
*Sachets can be any
shape. These butterflies
are simple to make and
quite charming.*

⌁ Suppliers ⌁

SUPPLIERS

Some have both a retail and a mail order business. Call for information.

MAIL ORDER SOURCES

for essences, fixatives, dried flowers and other potpourri ingredients

———⁂———

TOM THUMB
WORKSHOPS
Route 13, P.O. Box 357
Mappsville, VA 23407
(804) 824-3507
(Shop on the premises)

CAMBRIDGE
CHEMISTS, INC.
21 East 65th Street
New York, NY 10021
(212) 734-5678

CASWELL-MASSEY
CATALOG DIVISION
111 8th Avenue
Suite 1532
New York, NY 10011
(800) 326-0500

WELL-SWEEP HERB FARM
317 Mount Bethel Road
Port Murray, NJ 07865
908 (201) 852-5390
(Essential oils and fixatives)

RETAIL SOURCES

for essences, fixatives, dried flowers, and other potpourri ingredients

ANGELICA'S
TRADITIONAL HERBS
AND FOODS, INC.
147 First Avenue
New York, NY 10003
(212) 529-4335

APHRODISIA
282 Bleecker Street
New York, NY 10014
(212) 989-6440
(Catalog available)

CASWELL-MASSEY
58 Phipps Plaza
3500 Peachtree Road N.E.
Atlanta, GA 30326
(404) 261-9415

CASWELL-MASSEY
Copley Place
100 Huntington Avenue
Boston, MA 02116
(617) 437-9292

CASWELL-MASSEY
Pavilion at the Old
Post Office
1100 Pennsylvania
Avenue N.W.
Washington, DC 20004
(202) 898-1833

CASWELL-MASSEY
518 Lexington Avenue
New York, NY 10017
(212) 755-2254

CASWELL-MASSEY
Stonestown Galleria
3251 20th Avenue
San Francisco, CA 94132
(415) 681-1606

GILBERTIE'S HERB
GARDENS
Sylvan Lane
Westport, CT 06880
(203) 227-4175
(Herbs and
essential oils)

KIEHL'S
109 Third Avenue
New York, NY 10003
(212) 475-3698/
677-3171
(Essential oils)

❀ STORAGE JARS *These lovely jars contain potpourri. When put on display, the lids are removed to allow the fragrance to escape.*

❧ CONSERVATION OF WILD PLANTS ❧

THROUGH MY LOVE of gardening and my interest in the historical significance of our wild and cultivated plants, has grown an awareness of the threat that we pose to the survival of our environment. There must now be some redress to the balance of the intricate and fragile equilibrium of the natural world. Everyone can make some contribution toward this, and I hope that the contents of this book will encourage all those who read it to experiment with alternative ways of freshening and sweetening their homes. I also hope that it will stimulate an interest in natural beauty preparations. All these fragrant delights are biodegradable and pose no threat to the atmosphere.

When looking out of doors for wild flowers and plants suitable for drying for potpourri, it is wise to take along an illustrated guide book for identification of the flora you encounter. In the United States, there are over a hundred rare species of plants and flowers that are protected by law – and several thousand more in line to be protected. The laws differ from state to state but are particularly strong on Federal lands where penalties for removing plants can be heavy. Please be aware that a plant that is common in one region of the United States may be considered rare in another region and, therefore, protected by law.

To find out more about the wild plants and flowers that are protected in your area, you can consult reference books and directories at your local library, or contact a wildlife agency or regional office of the US Fish and Wildlife Service.

———— ❀ ————

❧ POISONOUS PLANTS ❧

TAKE GREAT CARE in gathering plants, flowers and berries. The fruits of the following woodland or garden plants are known to be poisonous to man and animals. Avoid using them in potpourri, no matter how attractive they might look. In addition to these specific plants, avoid picking any white fruits that you come across.

Common Name	Latin Name	Common Name	Latin Name
Black Locust	*Robinia pseudoacacia*	Mayapple, mandrake	*Podophyllum peltatum*
Castor-bean	*Ricinus communis*	Poison ivy	*Rhus radicans*
Common moonseed	*Menispermum canadense*	Poison sumac	*Rhus vernix*
Deadly nightshade	*Solanum dulcamara*	Pokeweed	*Phytolacca americana*
English ivy	*Hedera helix*	Spindle tree	*Euonymus europaea*
February daphne	*Daphne mezereum*	Wisteria	*Wisteria* spp.
Golden-chain	*Laburnum anagyroides*	Yews	*Taxus* spp.

———— ❀ ————

❧ INDEX ❧

ACKNOWLEDGMENTS

The author would like to thank all those at Dorling Kindersley who have worked so hard on this book. Jo Weeks, my editor, for her quiet enthusiasm and hard work; Caroline Mulvin, the designer, for her artistic contribution; Kate Grant for collecting my work and transporting it to London with such care, and Jane Laing and Alex Arthur for overseeing the project. Finally, a special thank you to my family, who always keep me going in moments of self doubt.

Dorling Kindersley would like to thank the following:

Lunn Antiques, New King's Road, London, for the lace pillow cases and nightdress case (pp.72-73), Owen Owen, Richmond, Surrey and The Reject China Shop, Regent Street, London, for crockery and cutlery. Germana Arthur for the linen press (p.56) and sundries kindly lent throughout the book, Lucinda and Emma Ganderton for assorted decorative bottles (pp.76-77, 102-3, 111),

Valerie and Heather Janitch for the lavender bundles (p.70), Deirdre and Mark Moloney for their teddy bear(p.86), Dodie Strasser for the easel (pp.28-29) and Hopscotch Props for the crib (p.86). Also thanks to Susan Thompson and Heather Dewhurst for editorial help, Pauline Bane for the illustrations, Peter Moloney for the index, Kate Grant for keying-in and Maryann Rogers for help with production.